MW01620466

Words Are Wonderful

An Interactive Approach to Vocabulary

Book 4

Dorothy Grant Hennings

Illustrations by John L. Garcia

EDUCATORS PUBLISHING SERVICE
Cambridge and Toronto

Acknowledgments

I would like to express my appreciation to the following people for their contributions to *Words Are Wonderful*:

- Teachers Megin Charner-Laird, Katie Charner-Laird, Deborah Henry, Joanna Kennedy, Nancy Martin, Cynthia Shermeyer, and Jan Wells for reviewing the first draft of the project and sharing their very useful suggestions.
- Charlie Heinle and Kate Moltz for their support and continued confidence in the project.
- Persis Barron Levy for her creative ideas for the overall design of the series.
- Wendy Drexler for her thoroughness in editing the manuscript, her overall management of the project, and her ideas for changes that strengthened the series.
- George Hennings, who urged and encouraged me to undertake this project and to see it through, for his critical reading of the manuscript in all its drafts, and for his work on the glossary.

—Dorothy Grant Hennings

Credits

p. 10, Dru Sefton, "Flaky Pics," from *The Star Ledger*, January 10, 2004. Used by permission of Newhouse News Service, Washington, D.C.

Glossary: George Hennings
Typesetting: Creative Pages, Inc.
Editor: Wendy Drexler
Managing Editor: Sheila Neylon

© 2005 by Educators Publishing Service, a division of School Specialty Publishing, a member of the School Specialty Family. All rights reserved. No part of this book may be reproduced or utilized in any form or by any electronic or mechanical means, including photocopying, without permission in writing from the publisher.

Printed in USA

ISBN 978-0-8388-2540-2

3 4 5 6 7 MLY 12 11 10 09 08

To George, who keeps on helping, caring, loving

Contents

Part 3

Part 4

Dear Student,

This is your book. In it you will learn how to figure out the meanings of words you do not know. You will learn to use the pictures in a book as clues to help you learn new words. You will learn to use words that you already know to help you understand unfamiliar words. You will learn how to use clues hidden inside words to figure out their meanings. What you will be doing is learning strategies that will help you read other books. A **strategy** is a way of figuring out things based on what you already know. It is a way of solving problems.

By reading this book, you will also increase the size of your **vocabulary**. It is important to have a large vocabulary. People who know many words can read faster, understand what they read, and speak and write more clearly.

To help your vocabulary grow, start a Vocabulary Notebook. In you notebook, you should have at least twenty-six pages—one page for each letter of the alphabet. Label each page with a letter of the alphabet in **alphabetical order** (for example, A a; B b; C c). When you finish each lesson in Book 4, pick three words you like from it. Record them in your notebook based on their first letter. Keep studying the words you have chosen. Use those words as you talk to your teacher and friends.

Words are truly wonderful, and I hope by the time you have read Book 4 of *Words Are Wonderful*, you will know why this is true. In this book, you will be introduced to amazing and powerful words that come from diverse languages, such as *hacienda* (from Spanish), *décor* (from French), *phenomenon* (from Greek), and *fauna* (from Latin). You will work with clusters of words that share a common kinship, such as *pressing, impress, impressive, suppress, depress, compress,* and *repressive*. You will build word towers, construct word webs, work crossword puzzles, and solve analogies. So have fun with words as you grow your vocabulary.

Sincerely,

Dorothy Grant Hennings

Part 1

Dictionary, Glossary, and Context Clues

Analyzing Words with Multiple Meanings

How are pearls and **oysters** related? Read to discover the connection between the shiny beads people wear as jewelry and oysters that live in, or reside in, grayish shells in the sea.

Pearls and Oysters

A pearl is a small **gem** that comes in a variety of white, pink, and gray **hues** and that has a special **luster**, or shine. It is the product of an oyster—a sea-dwelling organism that is a member of the scientific phylum Mollusca and the class Pelecypoda.[1] Oysters live in coastal regions of the world. They attach themselves to broken, decaying shells and the remains of other organisms that reside on the bottom of the sea.

All members of the phylum Mollusca are **invertebrates**. These creatures do not have backbones; instead, shells, or **valves**, support their soft bodies. Pelecypods are a kind of mollusk, or shelled organism; they are bivalves. This means that they have two shells. The meaning of *bivalve* is right there within the word: *Bi-* means "two," and in this context *valve* means "shell." Oysters have a flat lower shell and a larger, curved upper shell.

A **hinge** along one side of the shell connects the two valves of a Pelecypod just as a door is connected to a wall via a hinge. A bivalve uses the hinge to open its two shells and close them up tightly. It can literally "clam up." Oysters and other bivalves such as clams and mussels clam up to protect themselves from enemies that try to enter the bivalve's **residence** in search of a meal.

Not only are oysters encased in shells, but their soft bodies are also encircled within a membrane that surrounds them like a tent. This membrane is called a **mantle**. The outer surface of an oyster's mantle can secrete calcium-containing **crystals**. It does this to protect itself when an **irritant** of some kind slips between the mantle and the shell.

The irritant can be a grain of sand or any other small **particle**. The irritant bothers the oyster. To overcome the irritation caused by the particle, the

1. Scientists classify all organisms into groups based on common characteristics. A very large group of organisms that share a common feature is called a phylum. Subgroups of a phylum are called classes.

oyster surrounds the small piece of foreign matter with layer upon thin layer of calcium-carbonate crystals. The oyster does this because the speck of matter **irritates**, or annoys, it a lot. Years later, if you open an oyster that has laid down paper-thin layers of calcium-carbonate crystals, you will find a natural pearl.

Unfortunately, you would need to open as many as 10,000 oysters before finding one natural pearl. Fortunately, in the late 1800s in Japan, Kokichi Mikimoto began cultivating oysters and experimenting with different ways to trick, or **con**, them into producing pearls. Through his experiments, Mikimoto discovered that human beings could intervene in the process so that the oysters would more likely produce pearls.

What Mikimoto did was this. He taught Japanese divers to search for and **harvest** oysters along the seacoast. He then taught **technicians** how to place tiny calcium-carbonate seeds between the mantle and the shell of oysters that the divers had collected from the sea bottom. Technicians are specially trained workers who have learned a **technique**, or strategy, for performing a complicated task. Finally, he had the divers return the seeded oysters to the seabed in cages. He made sure that seawater always moved freely through the oyster beds. After about four years, Mikimoto reharvested the oysters. When technicians opened the bivalves, they found pearls inside. Today we call these kinds of pearls "cultured pearls" to distinguish them from natural pearls produced without **human intervention**. Not all pearls cultivated in this way are usable, but many are. As a result, today many people can afford to buy and wear pearls, and the production of cultured pearls has become a **lucrative** activity. It is highly profitable.

Thinking about Ideas and Relationships

1. How does a natural pearl differ from a cultured pearl? Use the phrase "human intervention" in your answer. If you have trouble using the phrase, check the meanings of *human* and *intervention* in the dictionary.

2. How do technicians contribute to the production of cultured pearls?

3. What is the function of the hinge found on Pelecypods?

Using a Dictionary to Investigate the Multiple Meanings of Words

1. Look up *valve* in your dictionary. Write three different meanings of the word.

    a.

    b.

    c.

2. Which meaning of *valve* relates to its use in the selection?

3. Look up *mantle* in your dictionary. Write three different meanings of *mantle.*

    a.

    b.

    c.

4. Which meaning of *mantle* defines *mantle* as used in the selection?

5. Look up *gem* in your dictionary. Write two different meanings of *gem*.

a.

b.

6. Which meaning of *gem* relates to its use in the first sentence of the selection?

7. Check the meanings of *hue* in your dictionary. Find the definition that relates to its use in the first paragraph of the selection and write it here.

8. What is a second meaning for the word *hue*? Give the meaning and then write a sentence with this meaning.

Using the Glossary to Find the Meanings of Words and Expressions

1. In the glossary, check the literal meaning of the phrase *to clam up*. What does an oyster do when it clams up?

2. *To clam up* also has a figurative meaning—a meaning that is a creative offshoot of the literal one. What does *clam up* mean in this sentence? *Because Marty knew he had already said too much, he clamed up for the rest of the discussion.* Use a dictionary to help you answer.

3. In the glossary, check the meanings of the noun *residence*. Find the definition of *residence* that relates to its use in paragraph three of the selection and write that definition here.

D Using Context Clues to Figure Out the Meanings of Words

Find the sentences in the selection where the words and expressions in the left column are used. From the way each word or expression is used, decide upon its meaning. Then put the letter of the correct definition on the line in front of the word.

Group One:

___ 1. luster — a. something that hurts or bothers one a lot

___ 2. invertebrate — b. shine

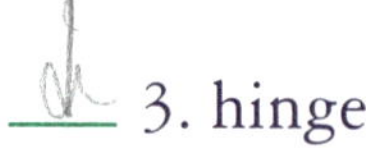
___ 3. hinge — c. an animal that does not have a backbone

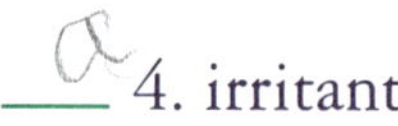
___ 4. irritant — d. a device that makes it possible for an object such as a door to close or turn

___ 5. technician — e. a person who is skilled in doing a particular job or task

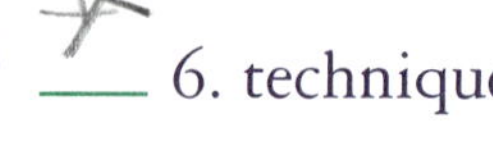
___ 6. technique — f. an action in which a person steps into a situation to change it in some way

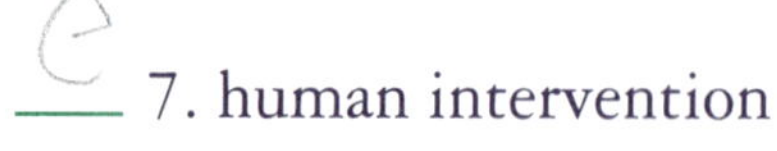
___ 7. human intervention — g. a systematic way of doing something

Group Two:

___ 8. harvest — h. profitable

___ 9. lucrative — i. to collect, as to collect wheat that is fully grown and ripe

___ 10. irritate — j. to trick

___ 11. particle — k. to bother or to cause pain

___ 12. con — l. a small piece or speck

STRATEGY CENTER

Look for clues to the meanings of an unfamiliar word by studying the context in which it is used. Check the dictionary or the glossary of a book when the context does not provide a clear clue to a word's meaning. Select the dictionary definition of the word that best fits the context.

Remember:

CDC

Check the **C**ontext; check the **D**ictionary; recheck the **C**ontext.

Revisiting *-Able* Words

Study the words *usable* and *profitable* in the last paragraph of the selection. Write down the meaning of the suffix *-able/-ible*: _______________. You should know the answer because you studied the suffix in Book 3 of *Words Are Wonderful*, and the meaning of the suffix is "right there" in the suffix itself.

1. What is the meaning of *usable*? Use word elements to help you answer.

2. What is the meaning of *profitable*? Use word elements to guide you. You can check the word *profit* in a dictionary if you need to.

3. Brainstorm other *-able* words. In your notebook, make a web of *-able* words. Place the suffix at the center of the web and write words with the suffix on strands extending outward.

Making Sense with the Key Words

Decide which word fits the context of each sentence. Then fill in the blank with that word.

crystals gem hues intervention irritates luster technique

1. A pearl is considered to be a beautiful ________________ because it has a wonderful ________________. It can be found in a variety of ________________—pink, white, and gray.

2. Some pearls are natural; they form when foreign matter happens to enter an oyster and ________________, or bothers, it a lot. Cultured pearls are the result of human ________________. Both natural and cultured pearls are made of ________________ of calcium carbonate.

3. Mikimoto perfected a ________________ for making cultured pearls.

clammed up conned harvest hinge intervening invertebrate irritant lucrative mantle residence Technicians valves

4. An oyster is an ________________ that has two ________________. The two shells are connected on one side by a ________________.

5. An oyster's primary ________________ is on the seabed in coastal waters.

6. ________________ slip a particle between the shell and the membrane of an oyster. Another name for the membrane is ________________. The piece of matter is an ________________ to the oyster, which then is returned to the sea. After four years or more, people ________________ the oyster to see if a pearl has formed.

7. By ________________ in this way, people can produce more pearls than can be found in nature. People have tricked, or ________________, the oyster into doing something it probably would not have done at that particular time.

8. Selling pearls can be a ________________ activity. People can get rich doing it.

9. When a person stops talking and won't say anything more on a topic, we say that he or she has ________________.

G Writing Workshop

Different kinds of animals live in shells. Investigate and write about the hermit crab, which resides in another animal's shell; the snail, which lives in a spiral-like shell; the abalone, which lives in an ear-shaped shell; or the turtle, whose residence is the shell on its back. In your report include the name that scientists use to refer to the creature, tell in what way the creature is unique, and explain where the creature lives. When you have finished your first draft, use a dictionary to check the spelling of three words in it. Be ready to show that you have checked the spelling in your report.

Synonyms, Shades of Meaning, and the Thesaurus

Analyzing Words with Multiple Meanings

Read the following diary entry to learn how photographers take pictures of snowflakes, or ice crystals.

Ice Crystals

This morning I awoke to find the earth blanketed under a layer of white. Snow had fallen during the night and had covered the land, the trees, the bushes, and the small plants. The bushes outside my window were so heavy with snow that their branches touched the ground. Large, wet masses, or clumps, of snow were falling from the trees and filled the air. The sun reflected off the snow, making it sparkle and shine with an **iridescence** that was unbelievably beautiful. The shine was even **lovelier** than the luster of pearls, for there were varied hues of the rainbow bouncing off the snow. The world was absolutely **gorgeous**. I don't remember ever seeing such a **magnificent** sight.

This afternoon, I saw an article in the local newspaper that explained the way photographers use photomicroscopy to take pictures of "**precariously** beautiful" single snowflakes. The article told about making photographs of those tiny crystals of ice through the lenses of a microscope. Photographers must use a microscope because the crystals are too small to be viewed with the human eye. The crystals are really **minuscule**—tinier than tiny.

The article explained that photographing snowflakes is "a **unique** art form that has been around since 1885, when one determined, nature-**passionate** Vermont farmer, Wilson Bentley, became the first person to take a magnified picture of one snowflake."[1] The article also explained that Bentley was the first person to **declare** that no two snowflakes are alike.[2]

I thought about how **extremely** difficult it must be to photograph delicate snowflakes and to capture their **exquisite**, six- or twelve-sided crystals on film. The crystals are "**fleeting** beauties," which means that they turn quickly into water if their temperature goes above their melting point of 0 degrees Centigrade. The problem is that photographers must **illuminate** what they are trying to record on film. Regular, round **incandescent** light bulbs give off a golden glow and **emit** heat, which melts the crystals. Photographers have learned

1. Dru Sefton, "Flaky Pics," *The Star-Ledger*, Saturday, January 10, 2004, page. 9.
2. "Flaky Pics," page 9.

to use “**banks** of **fluorescent** lights because they are cooler.”[3] Fluorescent tubes generally are long and produce a bluish light.

A second problem for photographers is that they must work in a very cold environment. They have to wear mittens to keep their hands warm, but these mittens are unique; the parts that cover their fingers can be pulled back to uncover their fingertips. This is important because photographers need to use their fingers to handle delicate equipment.

I’m just happy on this cold day that I can admire the snow from inside my house, and that I do not have to go outside and freeze my fingers.

3. “Flaky Pics,” page 17.

Thinking about Ideas and Relationships

1. What techniques do photographers use to take pictures of tiny ice crystals?

2. Why are ice crystals called “fleeting beauties”? Before answering, check the meaning of *fleeting* in a dictionary and reread the sentence in the selection that contains the phrase.

3. Why is a single snowflake “precariously beautiful”? Before answering, check a dictionary for the meanings of the words *precarious* and *precariously*. It may help you to remember that snowflakes are also fleeting.

4. The word *unique* means “being the only one, without an equal,” as well as “very unusual, extremely uncommon.” When we call something “unique,” we are saying that it is one of a kind—there is just nothing quite like it or equal to it. Think about the meaning of the root *uni-* in the word *unique,* and reread the two sentences in the selection where *unique* is used.

a. What do we mean when we say that photographing snowflakes is a *unique* art form?

b. What do we mean when we say that the mittens that photographers use to take pictures of ice crystals are *unique*?

c. Why would it be wrong to declare that something is very unique, or extremely unique? To answer, look carefully at the definition of *unique* in question 4.

Considering Synonyms and Shades of Meaning

1. In the selection, there are four synonyms for the word *beautiful: lovely, gorgeous, exquisite,* and *magnificent*. What general meaning do these words share?

2. Although *beautiful, lovely, gorgeous, exquisite,* and *magnificent* are synonyms, they differ somewhat in meaning, for synonyms do not mean "exactly the same." They are words that mean "almost the same." Among the words, there are slightly different **shades of meaning**. Refer to a dictionary to discover the special meaning and use of each of the words. Record your findings here.

   a. beautiful: ______

   b. lovely: ______

   c. gorgeous: ______

   d. exquisite: ______

e. magnificent:

____

3. How does the word *gorgeous* differ in meaning from the word *unique*?

4. How does the word *delicate* differ in meaning from the word *exquisite*? Check the context of the selection to see how the words are used and check the glossary for definitions.

STRATEGY CENTER

When you think about the meanings of synonyms, consider the particular shades of meaning that words carry.

C Completing Sentences

Finish each of the sentences started here. Before writing an answer, check a dictionary or the glossary for the meaning of the highlighted word. Also review the selection to discover the contexts in which the boldfaced words occur.

1. When someone **declares** something, he or she ______________________.
2. When someone declares something **passionately**, he or she ______________________
____.
3. If something has an **iridescent** shine, it ______________________
____.
4. If something is **minuscule**, it ______________________.
5. If a light bulb **emits** a lot of heat, it ______________________.

6. A **bank** of lights is ____.

7. A second meaning of the word *bank* is ______________________________.

8. A third meaning of *bank* is _____________________________________.

9. You should handle a **delicate** object ____________________________.

10. To **illuminate** something means to ______________________________.

Visualizing Ideas

1. Draw a picture of a typical **incandescent** light bulb.

2. Draw a picture of a **bank** of **fluorescent** light bulbs.

3. Draw a picture of something that is in a **precarious** position.

The Suffix *-Ment*

1. Study the words *equipment* and *environment* in the last paragraph of the article.

   What part of speech are they? _______________________________

2. Look up the suffix *-ment* in a dictionary. Starting with the examples given in the dictionary, create a web of *-ment* words in your notebook. Write the meaning of *-ment* in the center. Two good words to include are *judgment* and *government*.

F Reviewing the Highlighted Words 

Find the best definition for each word. Then write the letter of the definition on the line in front of the word. The first two lists contain adjectives, words we use to give more detail about nouns.

Group One: Adjectives

___ 1. minuscule	a. extremely excited about something; showing intense feeling
___ 2. gorgeous	b. very fine; easily broken
___ 3. unique	c. extremely beautiful
___ 4. passionate	d. extremely tiny
___ 5. delicate	e. without equal
___ 6. fleeting	f. passing swiftly; likely to last only a short time

Group Two: Adjectives

___ 7. lovely	g. in a dangerous position
___ 8. precarious	h. having great beauty
___ 9. magnificent	i. glowing with intense heat; very bright or clear
___ 10. incandescent	j. out of this world; absolutely great
___ 11. fluorescent	k. shining and giving off all the colors of the rainbow
___ 12. iridescent	l. almost perfect in form; having a delicate beauty
___ 13. exquisite	m. emitting cool, visible light

Group Three: Other Words

___ 14. iridescence	n. to give off
___ 15. illuminate	o. to say or state
___ 16. declare	p. to light up
___ 17. emit	q. very, very
___ 18. extremely	r. a shining brightness that contains all the hues of the rainbow

Writing Workshop

Write an account of a day in your life that was important to you. Or write about an idea or event about which you feel passionately. In your description, use words that carry a very positive meaning, or *connotation*. Words such as *lovely, gorgeous, magnificent*, and *exquisite* carry positive connotations. They are "feel good" words.

Connotation and Figurative Meanings

Understanding Formal and Informal Usages

West Africans weave stories about Anansi, the spider man, who was skilled at **trickery** and at pulling the wool over other people's eyes. A true "con artist," Anansi made a practice of **deceiving** others.[1] When West Africans were taken to Jamaica as slaves, they carried their tales of Anansi with them, and Jamaicans continue to enjoy the **clever** stories to this day. Read this story of Monkey and Tiger to see how **sly** Anansi **outwitted** both Monkey and Tiger to achieve his **selfish** ends.[2]

Monkey and Tiger

On Market Day, Monkey went to town and bought seven bananas, twelve mangoes, and four papayas. After making his **purchases**, Monkey worried about how he would **tote** everything back home. But Monkey did not feel **uneasy** for very long.

Behind him, Monkey heard a voice. It said, "Monkey, I will help you carry your things home." The voice belonged to Anansi, the spider man.

Monkey was **relieved.** He accepted Anansi's offer, and Monkey and Anansi started off together through the forest. As they rounded a bend, Monkey and Anansi heard someone calling out. It was Tiger! Monkey, who was a bit of a **simpleton,** knew enough to **panic.** Monkey meat is a staple in a tiger's diet. To a tiger, monkey meat is simply **delectable**—absolutely delicious. Although Monkey was **naive**, or easily taken in, he knew enough to be scared out of his wits when meeting a tiger. He was so frightened that he didn't know what to do, but at least he did not completely flip out.

In contrast, Anansi was a **crafty** chap. He knew how to get himself out of tight jams by hook or by crook, so he did not panic when he heard Tiger's voice. Instead, Anansi thought about how he might make the situation work for him.

1. The word *con* is a clipped form of the word *connive*, which means "to plot, to outwit, or to get the better of, someone else." The idea behind the words is not very nice.
2. Anansi is called the spider man because he was also very good at spinning tales. Some writers spell his name as *Ananse.*

Calmly, he called out to Tiger, "What's up, Tiger?"

Tiger replied, "I'm not up. I'm down. I have tumbled into this pit and I cannot get myself out. Throw me a rope."

Anansi didn't have a rope, but being **sly**, he hatched a **clever** but **nasty** plan to get rid of Monkey so he could have Monkey's fruit for himself. "Lower your tail into the hole, Monkey," he said, "so that Tiger can use it to pull himself up from the pit. I am helping you carry your purchases. Don't you want to help someone in return?"

Monkey was a **coward** as well as a simpleton, but he had a good heart. Quivering with fright, he lowered his tail into the pit, and Tiger grabbed hold with his powerful jaws. Of course, Anansi climbed up the nearest tree!

Up, up, and out of the hole came Tiger, holding Monkey's tail tightly in his mouth. When Tiger got to the top, he realized that what he thought was a rope was part of Monkey—and he loved monkey meat!

Monkey glanced up into the tree where Anansi was waiting to see what would happen next. After all, Anansi was a con man and he saw that his **scheme**—his clever plan—was working. He could almost taste those bananas, mangoes, and papayas, the fruit that Monkey had purchased. But at the last moment, Anansi took pity on Monkey and hatched another scheme.

"Tiger," he called, "What are you holding in your mouth?"

"Mon . . . ," Tiger replied. He could not speak clearly with a mouthful of monkey tail.

"Speak up, Tiger. Don't mumble. And don't you know that it is impolite to talk with your mouth full?"

Tiger fell for the trick. He opened his mouth and shouted, "I have a mouthful of Monkey." But to do that, Tiger had to open his mouth, and he had to drop Monkey's tail. In a flash, Monkey ran off.

Tiger looked up at Anansi and said, "Anansi, I should have remembered that you are a **trickster,** a con man, so **crafty** that you can **outwit** anyone. Next time I will keep my mouth shut." With that, Tiger took off after Monkey, but by then Monkey was halfway home.

When Tiger was out of sight. Anansi climbed down and gathered Monkey's forgotten fruit. "I really tricked both of them," Anansi said to himself. But you and I might wonder how anyone could enjoy something gotten by **foul,** rather than fair, means.

Thinking about Ideas and Relationships

1. What kind of man was Anansi? Would you want him for a friend? Use words from the story to describe him.

2. Why did Anansi offer to help Monkey tote his fruit home?

3. Why did Anansi tell Tiger that it was impolite to talk with his mouth full?

4. What kind of monkey was Monkey? Use words from the story to describe him.

5. Make a judgment: What was foul about what Anansi did?

Interpreting *Connotation*—the Positive or Negative Meaning of a Word

Some words send positive messages. For example, if I call someone "a prince" or "a princess," I am expressing my good feelings about him or her through the word I use—*prince/princess.* A word such as *prince, honey, gem, angel,* or *sugar* when used in reference to another person generally has an upbeat meaning, or a positive connotation. Other words that generally carry a positive connotation are *determined, brave,* and *neat.*

In contrast, people may have negative feelings that they connect, or associate, with some words. For example, if we angrily call someone "a rat," we are expressing our negative feelings about him or her. Linguists explain that a word such as *rat* when used in this way has a negative connotation. Other examples of words that may carry a negative connotation are *stubborn, foolhardy,* and *fussy.*

The dictionary meaning—stripped of all positive or negative associations—is a word's **denotation.** "A male member of a royal family" is the denotation of the word *prince.* "A little, gray, furry animal with a long tail" is the denotation of the word *rat.*

The following chart illustrates how synonyms can have positive or negative connotations.

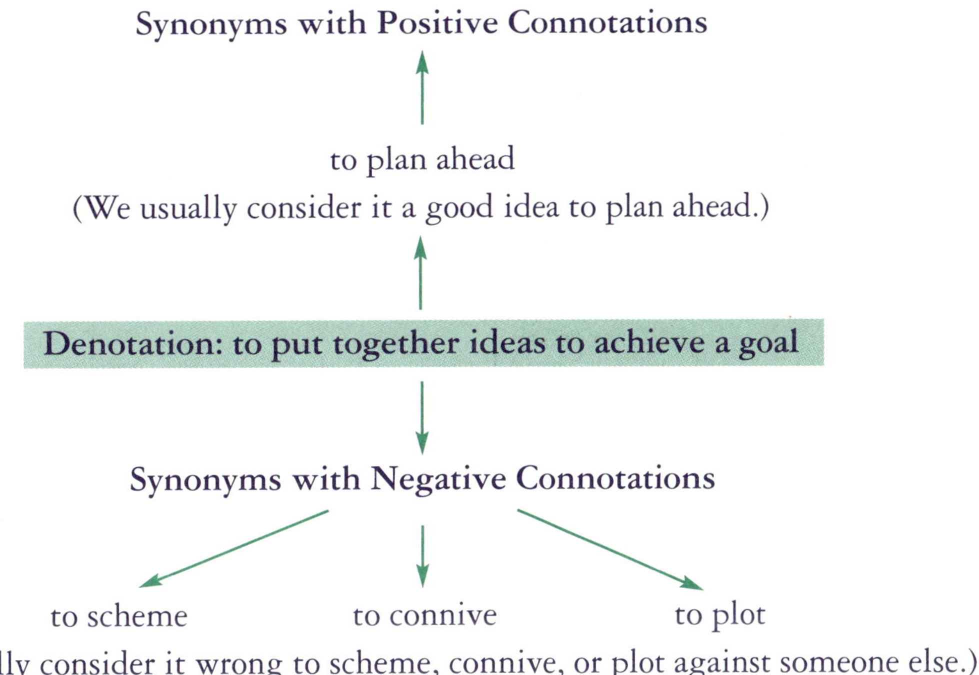

(We usually consider it wrong to scheme, connive, or plot against someone else.)

The words *scheme, connive,* and *plot* carry negative connotations. If you tell me that a person is scheming, conniving, or plotting against you, I would know that you feel uneasy about his or her actions. In contrast, if you say that the person was planning a course of action, you and I would feel more positive about the situation.

Similarly, the word *trickster* has a negative connotation. A trickster is someone who intentionally tries to fool someone else. Anansi was a trickster. None of us would want to be called a trickster. *Trickster* is not a nice word. In contrast, the word *helper* carries a positive connotation. We like the idea that people help other people.

Fill in the chart. Define the following words by studying how they are used in the story and/or by studying your dictionary. Then indicate whether each word carries a positive or negative connotation for you.

Words	Word Definitions	Word Connotations
1. sly		
2. relieved		
3. delectable		
4. clever		
5. nasty		

C Using Context and Glossary Clues to Distinguish Shades of Meaning

Match the words on the left with the correct definitions from the right. Place the letter of the correct definition on the line in front of each word. You can use context and dictionary clues. Be careful because some of the words are synonyms that have only slightly different shades of meaning.

Group One: Nouns

___ 1. purchases	a. someone who pulls the wool over someone else's eyes
___ 2. coward	b. a person who is very afraid to take action
___ 3. trickery	c. the act of pulling the wool over someone's eyes
___ 4. simpleton	d. things bought in a store or market
___ 5. trickster	e. a plan to do something, usually for a bad reason
___ 6. scheme	f. a person who does not know too much and does foolish things

Group Two: Verbs

___ 7. tote	g. to get the better of someone else by using greater intelligence
___ 8. panic	h. to pull the wool over someone's eyes; to mislead someone; to lie
___ 9. deceive	i. to be so frightened that a person doesn't know what to do
___ 10. outwit	j. to carry
___ 11. scheme	k. to plan to outwit someone, generally by foul rather than fair means
___ 12. relieved	l. to be freed from a burden; to be given relief

Group Three Words: Adjectives

___	13. delectable	m. easily fooled or tricked; lacking worldly experience
___	14. uneasy	n. thinking mainly of oneself
___	15. selfish	o. sly
___	16. crafty	p. not comfortable with events or circumstances
___	17. nasty	q. not nice
___	18. foul	r. really nasty; very wicked; vile
___	19. naive	s. delicious; delightful

STRATEGY CENTER

As you listen and read, look for positive and negative meanings embedded in the passage. Often a speaker or writer will intentionally use words with negative or positive connotations to help you recognize, or make you agree with, his or her point of view.

D Distinguishing between Formal and Informal Expressions

We use some words mainly in talking informally with friends. Some of these expressions are called "slang." Some are idioms. We don't use those words in writing an important essay or giving a serious speech. For example, the verb *to con* is slang, whereas the synonyms *to mislead* or *to deceive* are more acceptable in formal situations. In the article are some expressions we use primarily in informal situations. Use the context of the article to determine the meanings of these expressions. Write the intended meanings in the space provided or draw a picture if you prefer.

1. to pull the wool over people's eyes

2. to round a bend

3. to be scared out of one's wits

4. to have a good heart

5. to hatch a scheme

6. to fall for a trick

7. to take off

8. in a flash

9. to clam up

10. to flip out

STRATEGY CENTER

When you write and speak, remember to reserve slang expressions for informal situations.

Writing with Words and Expressions

Use these words and expressions in sentences. You may put more than one word in a sentence. Record your sentences in your notebook.

naive	simpleton	coward	pull the wool over his eyes
deceive	tote	purchases	hatch a scheme
crafty	outwit	delectable	by hook or by crook
trickery	uneasy	by fair or foul means	

F Writing Workshop

Write a story that depends on trickery, craftiness, and deception. To make your story effective, make one of your characters a sly trickster like Anansi and the other character a naive character like Monkey. A distinct contrast between characters helps establish the conflict in a story.

Multiple Meanings and the Word Element Mini-

Reading and Writing Biography

Read the following biographical account to discover how one researcher has earned the name "The Elephant Woman."

Cynthia Moss—The Elephant Woman

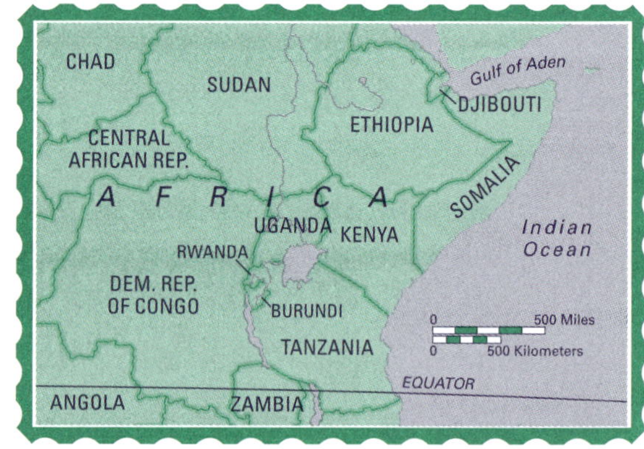

Imagine sitting in an old Land Rover when a bull elephant that weighs more than 14,000 pounds **charges** your vehicle. As the mighty male elephant rushes directly at you, you would probably be even more frightened than Cynthia Moss was when a bull elephant charged her.

Cynthia Moss is a researcher who lives in a tented camp on the plains of Kenya in East Africa. The camp has only **minimal** facilities. Living under very simple conditions, Moss spends most of her time observing the activities of elephants in Amboseli National Park. She makes notes based on her observations and takes photographs to **document** what she sees.

When Moss was interviewed recently, she talked about her **encounter** with Bad Bull, the largest male elephant living in Amboseli. "He sort of **ambushed** me," she said during the interview. "He hid behind a palm tree and came rushing out, charging our vehicle. We only just got away." Moss explained to her interviewer that she generally gives Bad Bull "**a wide berth.**"[1] She keeps her distance because Bad Bull has "a nasty **disposition.**" He has caused, or **wreaked,** a lot of **havoc** in the region—destruction that Moss and her fellow researchers can do without.

Through her research, Cynthia Moss has learned a great **deal** about elephant behavior. She has learned that no two elephants are **identical.** She can tell elephants apart by their **distinctive** features, such as the shape of their ears. Based on the clear differences that she sees, Moss assigns names to the elephants she studies. If you visit her camp, she will refer to "her" elephants by name, for example, Ebony, Ely, Enid, Edwina—all children, or **offspring,** of Echo and members of the E-family.

1. Marge Mueller, "An Interview with Cynthia Moss, November 1, 1999. Go to http://elephant.elehost.com for the complete interview (accessed October 4, 2004).

Moss has learned that elephants live together in family, or **kinship,** groups. The leader of a family is the most senior adult female in that group. Echo's family—the E-family—includes her adult female children and the young offspring of those elephants, both male and female. However, when male elephants are about 14 years old, they leave the family. They become **loners,** who wander the plains on their own.

Several years ago, I was with a group of tourists who visited Cynthia Moss in her camp in Kenya. As we sat on the ground listening to her talk, a family of elephants **lumbered** into the camp, stood in a group, and looked us over. Moss identified the female leader. She named the adult female offspring and their children and explained how the elephants were related to one another—their kinship. As the elephants plodded heavily and noisily toward us, I was **overwhelmed.** Overcome by their size and a little scared, I climbed into our minivan. But Cynthia Moss was quick to tell us that the danger was minimal.

Cynthia Moss loves the elephants of Amboseli and is concerned about the havoc wreaked by people who enter the **game** reserve illegally to **poach.** Poachers kill elephants for their ivory tusks. Recently, when a local warrior speared Elephant Erin, Moss stayed with her around the clock until she died. As Moss explained, "This was a female we knew so well. She was in so many ways like an old friend and to see her in pain was almost unbearable."

Moss reported that the other elephants in Erin's family kept returning to be with their dying sister. They, too, were saddened by their relative's death. As Moss concluded, the elephants have a "large network of relationships, probably larger than any other land mammal." They have **complex** social lives that make them very special creatures.[2]

2. These quotations are from the notebooks of Cynthia Moss. Go online to www.elephanttrust.org (accessed October 4, 2004).

Thinking about Ideas and Relationship

1. Why is Cynthia Moss called "The Elephant Woman"?

2. Retell the story of Moss's encounter with Bad Bull. Use the words *ambushed, charged, disposition,* and *wreaked havoc* in your explanation.

3. What has Moss learned about elephants? Use the words *identical, distinctive, kinship,* and *offspring* in your answer.

4. If Moss worked with a B-family of elephants, what names might she assign to animals in this kinship group?

B Interpreting Words with Multiple Meanings

Some words have more than one meaning. Fill in the circle next to the answer that gives the definition of the word as used in the selection about Cynthia Moss.

1. charge

   Ⓐ to accuse someone of something, as to charge someone with a crime

   Ⓑ to postpone payment, as when someone charges something on his or her credit card

   Ⓒ to set a price, as when a storeowner charges a dollar for an orange

   Ⓓ to rush forward to attack

2. lumber

   Ⓐ to move or walk heavily with a rumbling noise

   Ⓑ wood sawed into boards

3. game

   Ⓐ wild animals that are hunted for food or other reasons

   Ⓑ a competitive activity such as football

   Ⓒ a form of amusement, such as a game of cards

4. deal

Ⓐ to hand out playing cards

Ⓑ to do business with, as in the sentence, "I will deal only with honest people."

Ⓒ to handle, or consider, as in the sentence, "I can only deal with one problem at a time.

Ⓓ a favorable bargain, as in the expression, "What a deal!"

Ⓔ an amount, as in the sentence, "He had a great deal of experience working with machines."

5. poach

Ⓐ to cook in boiling water, as when someone poaches eggs

Ⓑ to go on someone else's land illegally to hunt and kill game

6. document

Ⓐ a written piece of paper that provides official proof of something

Ⓑ to support, or give good evidence in support of; to make a record of

C Dealing with *Mini*words

A minibike is a little bicycle. A minivan is a little van. A miniskirt is a very short skirt. A television miniseries is a small group of programs, usually on the same topic.

1. What is the meaning of the word element *mini-*? Decide based on its use in the sentences above.

2. What is true of sites where there are only minimal facilities, as was the case in Moss's tented camp?

3. A brochure reads, "This program will be held only if a minimum of ten people sign up." What does that mean? Base your answer on what you know about the meaning of *mini-*.

4. Your father tells you, "Don't minimize the value of going to college. A college education can help you get ahead." What does a person do if he or she minimizes the value of something?

D Defining Words Based on Clues "Right There" in a Selection

Next to each word or phrase, write down words from the selection that are clues to its meaning.

1. charge: ______________________________

____

2. ambush: ______________________________

____

3. a wide berth: ______________________________

____

4. offspring: ______________________________

____

5. no two elephants are identical: ______________________________

____

6. overwhelmed: ______________________________

____

7. loner: ______________________________

____

8. havoc: ______________________________

____

9. distinctive features: ______________________________

____

10. kinship: ______________________________

____

11. wreaked: ______________________________

____

Using a Dictionary or Glossary to Confirm the Meanings of Words

Look up the following words in a dictionary or the glossary of this book. Complete the data chart based on your findings.

Words	Dictionary Definitions Related to the Use of the Words in the Selection	Sentences Using the Words
1. complex (adjective)		
2. disposition (noun)		
3. encounter (noun)		

Select the word that best fits the context of the sentence and write that word in the blank.

Group One

berth charge disposition encounter kinship loners offspring overwhelmed

1. Marty's dog has a mean ________________. Because of that, when I ____________ the dog, I give him a wide ___________. Actually, I am afraid that he may ____________ me. I am also __________________ by the dog's immense size.

2. Elephants live in groups that are related through ____________. Female elephants keep their ____________ near them, especially when their children are young. Older males become ____________, roaming the plains on their own.

Group Two

ambush complex deal distinctive document identical lumbered minimal poachers

3. Careful researchers ________________ their findings by recording what they have learned in their notebooks.

4. People are more likely to believe in the accuracy of the information when two researchers get ________________ results.

5. Research can be very ____________. Researchers may have to deal with many different problems. But by being very careful, researchers can learn a great ____________.

6. The elephants ____________________ down the path. They did not know that ____________________ were hiding in the bushes, waiting to ______________ them.

7. The poachers expected to find the elephants with __________________ effort. They discovered, however, that they had to work harder than they had thought.

8. All elephants have ________________ characteristics so that a researcher can tell one animal from another.

Write sentences using the following phrases.

1. wreaked havoc

2. gave a wide berth to

Writing Workshop

The biographer who wrote about Cynthia Moss did not start by telling about Moss's birth, where she grew up, or where she went to school. Instead, she began with Moss's encounter with Bad Bull. This was the hook that the biographer used to make the introduction more interesting. When you write a report or story, try writing several beginnings and keep in mind that you want to interest people in reading your story. Then choose the hook that best catches people's attention. You may want to write a biography of Jane Goodall, who studied apes in West Africa, or Marie Curie, a scientist who discovered two elements.

Homophones, Commonly Confused Words, and the Elements Mid- and Rupt-

Interpreting Proverbs and Other Colorful Expressions

Locate Iceland on a globe or map of the Western Hemisphere. Based on its location, hypothesize what you would expect to find if you visited there. Then read the selection to find out whether your hypothesis was correct.

Iceland, Land of Fire and Ice

Are you interested in visiting a unique country—one located farther west than any other land in Europe? If **you're** interested, let me **counsel**, or advise, you to go to Iceland.

Iceland is in the North Atlantic Ocean about **midway** between the continental mass of Europe and the North American continent. It is so far north that the average high temperature for July is 58 degrees Fahrenheit. But that does not mean that everything is brown, barren, and cold. Iceland is a green land of **geysers** that **periodically erupt,** sending spouts of steam and hot water upward into the air.

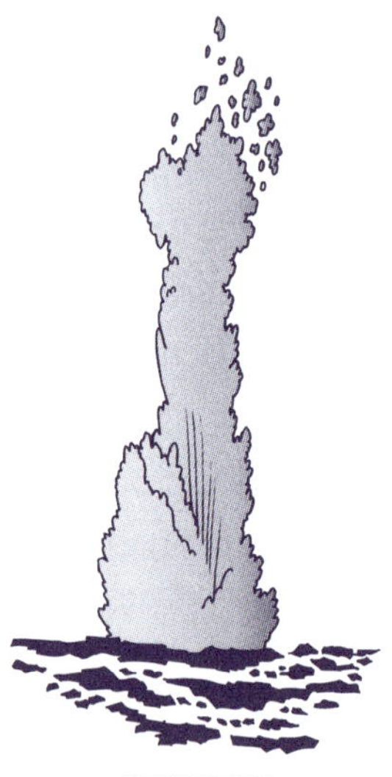
geyser

A trip to Iceland would be **worthwhile** just to see the geysers, **except** that **there** are even more interesting things to see there. Iceland is the **site** of volcanoes that from time to time erupt and send molten rock through vents, or **holes,** in the earth upward to the surface. It is also a land of lagoons—shallow pools of water that in Iceland stay naturally at 106 degrees Fahrenheit even on the coldest days. If you go to Reykjavik,[1] the capital of Iceland, you will see Icelanders swimming in the steaming Blue Lagoon, a main tourist attraction. Icelanders also use the water that collects in hot spring **reservoirs** to heat their buildings.

Although Iceland is **principally** known for its natural sites, it is also known for **its** people. Icelanders tend to be easygoing and informal. They respect one another as **peers** and are proud of **their heritage.** One part of their background that **they're** especially proud of is their legislature, the Althing. The oldest governing **council** in the world, the Althing was founded in 930 AD.

1. The pronunciation of Reykjavik is **Rā´kyə vik´.**

Clearly, their midocean position just south of the Arctic Circle **affects** the Icelanders. This is the Land of the Midnight Sun. In June the sun shines almost twenty-four hours per day; it shines even at midnight. I counsel you to visit then, for in the winter months, **it's** just the opposite—almost twenty-four hours of darkness.

Most Icelanders **accept** the **effects** of their northern location. They seem to believe in the principle "to live and let live."[2] Their idea of not holding grudges and forgetting past insults may be an outcome of spending **whole** days almost in the dark during the winter season. However, it does not feel so dark in Iceland during the winter because the Icelanders themselves shine all winter long. They appear to enjoy life no matter what the season.

When visitors arrive in Iceland, they easily join in the good, plain fun. They take a dip in the Blue Lagoon, enjoy a special meal called a "smorgasbord," and have a blast. They visit the geysers, the waterfalls, the farms, the glaciers, and the magnificent mountain areas.

But an important tip to travelers anywhere is not to do anything in **excess.** Don't **overdo** it. Don't go overboard with the fun. And if you travel to a faraway place, remember that you are a visitor and that the people living there have allowed you **access** to their town, city, or country.

2. Expressions such as "live and let live" are also called "proverbs." A **proverb** is a short, wise saying. Proverbs are part of our heritage. They have been passed down from one generation to the next, from parents to their children. Another example of a proverb is "the early bird catches the worm." A synonym for the word *proverb* is *maxim.*

A Thinking about Ideas and Relationships

1. Complete the web given here. In the center, record the topic of the essay, which you can find by reading the title. Then add information about the location, geographic features, and the people based on what you learned from the essay.

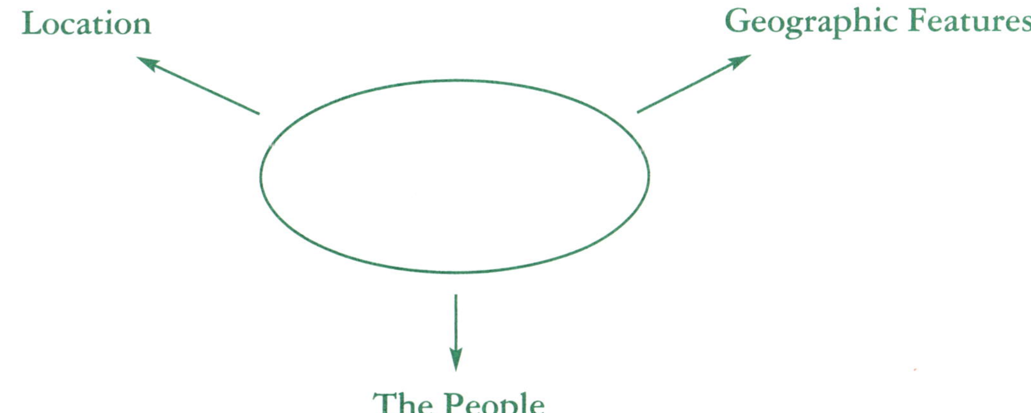

2. What do we mean when we say that Icelanders tend to be easygoing people?

3. **Cite** one fact from the selection that documents the idea that Icelanders have a heritage to be proud of.

Reviewing Common Homophones

Homophones are words that are pronounced the same but differ in spelling and meaning. In Books 1 and 2 of *Words Are Wonderful,* you studied the homonym sets *they're, there,* and *their; it's* and *its; you're* and *your;* and *site* and *sight.* Read the following sentences, decide which homophone fits the context of each sentence and complete the sentences. Use context and dictionary clues as well as what you already know to help you answer.

They're, there, their; It's, its; you're, your; site, sight

1. Tell me when ____________ going on your trip so that I can give you a going-away present.
2. "Martha," I said, "____________ gloves are on the table."
3. When Martha did not find her gloves ____________ on the table, I helped her look for them.
4. "____________ right there," I told her. "Can't you see them?"
5. Jose and Angelica gave ____________ parents a gift because they appreciated what they had done for them.
6. "____________ starting to snow," Brad told me. "You had better go home early."
7. The cat washed ____________ paws after eating supper.
8. Iceland is the ____________ of many glaciers as well as volcanoes and hot springs.
9. Because my eye____________ is poor, I have to wear contact lenses.

The word *cite* is pronounced the same way as *site* and *sight* but has a different meaning. Study these sentences.

- Good authors **cite,** or mention, the reference books they have used to get information.
- **Cite** a fact from the article that supports your hypothesis.
- I will **cite** one more example to help you better understand my point of view.

10. What is the meaning of the word *cite* as used in these sentences? Check your answer in a dictionary before writing a definition and another sentence using the word.

C Dealing with More Homophones and Other Confusing Words

Here are the definitions of more homophones and some commonly confused words. Select the word that fits best in each sentence based on its definition and the context in which the word is used in the essay. Write the correct word on the line.

Group One: Homophones

principal *(adjective)*, main, most important.

principal *(noun)*, a person who is the head of a school.

principle *(noun)*, an idea on which a person bases his or her actions; a rule of action.

related word: principally *(adverb)*, mainly.

1. The teacher followed this ____________________: Think before you act.
2. The ____________________ reason Jeff failed the test was that he did not study.
3. The teacher consulted the ____________________ before she made a decision.
4. The teacher was ____________________ concerned about making the rules fair for everyone.

Group Two: Homophones

peer *(noun)*, a person who is equal in some way to another person.

pier *(noun)*, a dock where ships tie up.

hole *(noun)*, an opening; a vent.

whole *(adjective)*, entire.

5. The ship docked at the ____________ and the passengers got off, or disembarked.

6. During the party, we ate the ____________ birthday cake.

7. James and I dug a large ____________ in the backyard and planted an apple tree.

8. My co-worker and I are both equally skilled at what we do. She is my ____________.

Group Three: Homophones

council *(noun),* a group of people elected to make laws.

counsel *(verb),* to advise.

counsel *(noun),* a lawyer; advice given.

9. Brian's goal was to serve on the town ____________. To do that, he had to put his name on the ballot at election time.

10. Ms. Ramero was the chief ____________ for the defense during the trial.

11. Her ____________ to her client was always very thoughtful.

Group Four: Commonly Confused Words

accept *(verb),* to take what someone has offered.

except *(preposition)*, other than; were it not for.

access *(noun),* the right to enter or approach; admittance.

excess *(noun),* an amount greater than normal.

affect (*verb*), to influence; to have an effect on; to act on the emotions of.

effect (*noun*), the result; the outcome.

12. ____________ for Josh's insistence on completing the job by himself, we would all have stayed to help him.

13. My teacher gave me this counsel: Don't do anything in ____________. Don't go overboard. Take the middle-of-the-road approach.

14. Kate wanted _____________ to the fair grounds, but she didn't have enough money to pay the entrance fee.

15. Chelsea was too proud to _____________ the money from me although I was willing to give it to her.

16. How will his getting elected ___________ Brian's life? Will it change how he lives? I don't know what the _____________ will be. Only time will tell.

D Dealing with the Prefix *Mid-*

You probably know the meaning of the word *middle. Middle* means "in the center, halfway between two points." There are a number of other words built from the prefix *mid-* that also communicate the idea of being between two points. Answer these questions based on your understanding of the principal word element.

1. If you come to a midway point, where are you?

2. If a car is midsized, what is true about it?

3. If an island has a midocean location, where would you expect to find it?

4. When is it midday compared to midnight?

5. How old will you be when you are in your midteens?

6. When is midweek?

E Writing Sentences with New Words

Use context and dictionary clues to complete these sentences. At the end of each item is a clue that may help you understand the boldfaced word.

1. **Periodically** means from ____.
   (Periodically relates to a period of time.)

2. When a **geyser erupts,** it ____.
   (A related word is *eruption.*)

3. A **reservoir** is a place where ______________________________.
(A related expression is "to keep something in reserve.")

4. **Worthwhile** things to do are ______________________________.
(*Worthless* is a word that is opposite in meaning.)

5. When people talk about their **heritage**, they are referring to ______________
______________________________.
(People inherit things from their parents and culture.)

6. When you **overdo**, you ______________________________.
(Note the word *do* in *overdo.*)

7. An **overdue** book is one that ______________________________.
(Note the word *due* in *overdue.*)

8. When a person **goes overboard,** he or she ______________________________.
(Compare *overboard* to *onboard* and *aboveboard.*)

9. To **take a dip** in the ocean means to ______________________________.
(This is a figurative use of words, not a literal use.)

10. If you believe in the **principle** of **"live and let live,"** you believe that __________
______________________________.
(Hear the alliteration in "live and let live.")

F Writing with Homophones and Commonly Confused Words

In your notebook write sentences with the following words. Try to include context clues to show that you know the differences in meaning among these sets of homophones and commonly confused words:

principal/principle	**site/sight/cite**	**their/there/they're**
hole/whole	**peer/pier**	**its/it's**
affect/effect	**council/counsel**	**accept/except**

Showing Your Understanding of New Words and Expressions

Write the letter of the definition on the line in front of the word or expression that is closest in meaning.

Group One Words

___ 1. erupt	a. halfway; in a middle position
___ 2. geyser	b. to break out; to burst up
___ 3. worthwhile	c. a spring from which a stream of water periodically comes up out of the earth
___ 4. reservoir	d. to do something in excess, beyond what is good for you
___ 5. heritage	e. traditions, values, and possessions handed down from one generation of people to the next
___ 6. overdo	f. a short, wise saying, such as "a stitch in time saves nine"
___ 7. proverb	g. a place where something is stored
___ 8. midway	h. of value

Group Two Expressions

___ 9. go overboard	i. forgive and forget
___ 10. take a dip	j. go for a swim
___ 11. live and let live	k. do things in excess
___ 12. have a blast	l. have a great time

H Writing Workshop

Here are some unique places that would be worthwhile to study or visit: Hiroshima, Japan; Xian, China; Bangkok, Thailand; Istanbul, Turkey; and Manaus, Brazil. Investigate what is unique about one of these places by accessing the Web or reading in an online or hardcover encyclopedia. Then write a short report on the interesting things found there. You might want to organize your report using the pattern in the essay about Iceland: an introduction in which you cite the location of the place, several paragraphs about the geographical features, and several paragraphs about the people. To help you gather data for your report, weave a web as in Activity A.

Reviewing What You Know
Lessons 1—5: Power Words Based on the Greek Suffixes -Ician, -Ism/-Ist, and -Logy/-Logist

Dealing with Multiple Meanings

Read the definitions of the word *senior* in column 1 and the sentences in column 2. On the line in front of each sentence, write the number of the definition that fits the meaning of the sentence. The part of speech is an important clue.

Definitions

1. the older of two men—a father and a son—who both have the same name, such as George senior and George junior (adjective)
2. older, elder, such as a senior citizen (adjective)
3. of a higher position; higher in rank (adjective)
4. a student in the last year of high school or college (noun)
5. related to the last year of high school or college (adjective)

___ a. Ricardo is in his **senior** year at the University of Southern California.

___ b. Although Jennifer is only a freshman in high school, she looks forward to the time when she will be a **senior.**

___ c. The **senior,** or oldest, female elephant in a herd is generally the leader of the family.

___ d. John Bronowski, **Senior,** is the father of John Bronowski, Junior. The grandson of John Bronowski, Senior, is John Bronowski III.

___ e. Ms. Agassi is a **senior** partner in a well-known law firm. She holds the highest position in the company.

B Dealing with More Words with Multiple Meanings

Find the phrase that gives the meaning of the boldfaced word as used in the sentence. Then fill in the circle in front of your answer.

1. I saw a large rhinoceros **lumbering** down the path in the grasslands of East Africa.

   Ⓐ moving heavily and noisily

   Ⓑ processing wood to make boards

2. "What a great **deal!**" my father exclaimed when he realized that he would be paying only half the listed price for a cell phone.

   Ⓐ handle or consider

   Ⓑ distribute cards

   Ⓒ amount

   Ⓓ bargain

3. Many people today use a credit card **to charge** products and services they buy.

   Ⓐ to run toward with violence in mind

   Ⓑ to set a price on

   Ⓒ to re-energize a battery

   Ⓓ to delay payment on a purchase

4. Nadeem took out some eggs and started **to poach** them.

   Ⓐ to go onto someone's land to take game illegally

   Ⓑ to cook something by boiling in hot liquid

5. In Jeff's house, there is a clock sitting on the **mantel.**

   Ⓐ a shelf over the fireplace

   Ⓑ a loose, sleeveless cloak worn over other clothes

   Ⓒ the part of a mollusk that secretes the shell

   Ⓓ a part of the earth that is just beneath the crust

6. Before going outside, my mother put on a **mantle** that covered her like a tent.

Ⓐ a shelf over the fireplace

Ⓑ a loose, sleeveless cloak worn over other clothes

Ⓒ the part of a mollusk that secretes the shell

Ⓓ a part of the earth that is just beneath the crust

7. The technician opened an important **valve** to release pressure so that there would not be an explosion.

Ⓐ a part that controls the flow of a liquid or gas through a pipe

Ⓑ a part of the heart that regulates blood flow

Ⓒ the shell of a mollusk

Ⓓ a device on some musical instruments that controls air flow

8. Patricia is a **gem.** She is the best friend I have.

Ⓐ a precious stone such as a diamond

Ⓑ a person who is well loved and highly valued

9. It is illegal to hunt the **game** in the state park.

Ⓐ animals that live wild in nature

Ⓑ a competitive activity

Ⓒ an entertaining activity

Dealing with Homophones and Commonly Confused Words

First, give the definition of the word *homophone*:

Next, pick the word from this list that best fits each context. Write the correct word on each line.

accept, except; access, excess; affect (verb), effect (noun); council, counsel; hole, whole; overdo, overdue; peers, piers; principal, principle; site, sight, cite

1. Bradford is going to visit the ____________ where the new high school is being built. Now there is only a large ____________ in the ground where the basement will be.
2. Don't ____________ it when you exercise. If you push yourself too hard, you will be sore the next day.
3. In some democracies, citizens have the right to a trial before a jury composed of their ____________.
4. You must be elected if you want to have a position on the town ____________.
5. The person who receives the smallest number of votes must ____________ the fact that he or she has lost the election.
6. What do you think will be the ____________ on the candidate if he loses the election? How do you think the loss will ____________ him?
7. I believe in the ____________ of giving help to other people who are in need.
8. Unless you buy a ticket, you will be denied ____________ to the fair.

Perceiving Kinship among Words

The words in each group are related in some way. In the space provided, indicate how the words are related. Be specific. Identify the element, the meaning of the element, and if you can, how the words relate to the element. The first one has been done for you.

1. miniseries, minimum, minimal

The words all contain the word element mini, *meaning "small." A* miniseries *is a small series,* minimum *means "a small amount," and* minimal *means "the least possible."*

2. midpoint, middle, midway

3. erupt, corrupt, disrupt

4. overdo, overdue, oversee

5. gratefully, recently, nastily

6. equipment, enjoyment, judgment

7. capable, profitable, desirable

Working with Connotation

As you have learned, we have more positive feelings about some words than about other words. Words that we view in an upbeat way have a positive connotation. Those that we view negatively have a negative connotation. Rewrite the words in each group, in order, from the word that has the most negative connotation on the left to the word that has the most positive connotation on the right.

1. courteous impolite rude

2. crafty sly shrewd smart clever

3. happy sorrowful depressed excited

4. dislike like love hate

Write one word that to you has a positive connotation: ______________________

Write one word that to you has a negative connotation: ______________________

Reviewing New Vocabulary

Write the letter of the definition on the line in front of the correct word.

Word List One: Nouns

___ 1. luster	a. the place where one lives
___ 2. hinge	b. color
___ 3. invertebrate	c. a small piece
___ 4. hue	d. a device that allows two connected parts to swing back and forth
___ 5. particle	e. an animal without a backbone
___ 6. residence	f. the shine of something

Word List Two: Verbs

___ 7. irritate	g. to give advice to
___ 8. harvest	h. to annoy
___ 9. intervene	i. to light up
___ 10. illuminate	j. to boil over
___ 11. erupt	k. to come between others in a situation
___ 12. counsel	l. to gather in, as when one gathers in crops

Word List Three: Adjectives

___ 13. naive	m. valuable
___ 14. complex	n. very complicated, with many different parts
___ 15. worthwhile	o. unique
___ 16. distinctive	p. sly
___ 17. crafty	q. unaware and trusting; likely to be taken in or conned
___ 18. foul	r. bad

Figuring Out Analogies

In Books 2 and 3 of *Words Are Wonderful*, you learned how to deal with analogies. An analogy expresses a relationship between two sets of words. Study the following analogy. Which word completes the analogy? Write that word on the line.

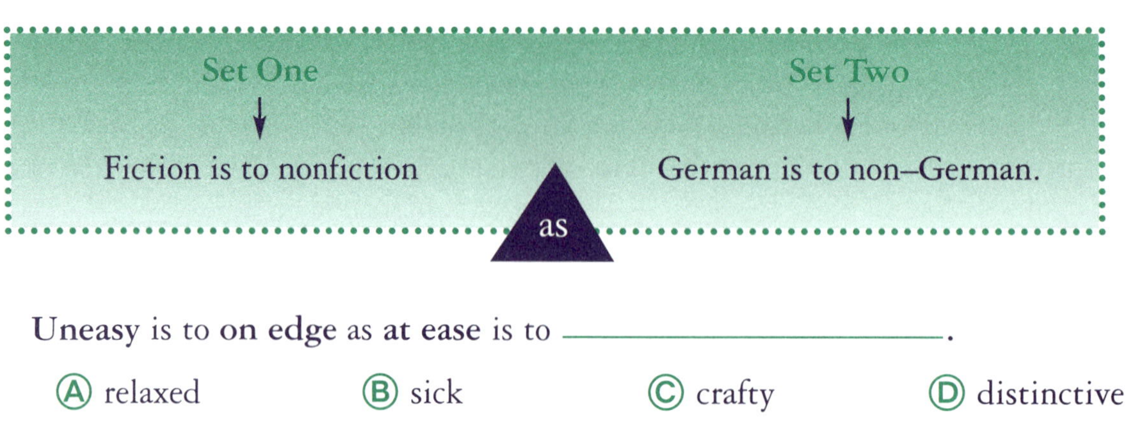

Uneasy is to **on edge** as **at ease** is to ______________.

Ⓐ relaxed Ⓑ sick Ⓒ crafty Ⓓ distinctive

To figure out the analogy, you must look at the two items in Set One and decide how they are related. In this case, you would probably say to yourself, "*Uneasy* means the same thing as the phrase *on edge.*" The words in Set Two must be related in the same way. In this case, both words must mean the same thing. Which word means the same as the phrase *at ease*? Obviously, the answer is a, *relaxed.*

Sometimes a colon (:) and a double colon (: :) take the place of the connecting words in an analogy. When you see a single colon, say to yourself the words *is to.* When you see the double colon, say the word *as.* Write the correct word on the line in the following example.

Ⓐ head Ⓑ skin Ⓒ feet Ⓓ arms

How are *oyster* and *shell* related? A shell is the covering on an oyster. What covers a person? The answer is skin, which is the covering on a person.

Complete the following analogies by filling in the circle in front of the best answer.

1. **lucrative : profitable : : precarious :** ____________

   Ⓐ dangerous Ⓑ easygoing Ⓒ precious Ⓓ worthwhile

2. **trickster : con man : : offspring :** ____________

   Ⓐ heritage Ⓑ loner Ⓒ scam Ⓓ children

3. **geyser : erupts : : counselor :** ____________

   Ⓐ inherits Ⓑ governs Ⓒ advises Ⓓ accepts

4. **ship : pier : : plane :** ____________

   Ⓐ airport Ⓑ ocean Ⓒ berth Ⓓ midpoint

5. **they're : they are : : it's :** ____________

   Ⓐ its Ⓑ it is Ⓒ their Ⓓ there

6. **minimum : least amount : : maximum :** ____________

   Ⓐ greatest amount Ⓑ smallest amount Ⓒ tallest kind Ⓓ most senior

Part 2

The Old English Prefix *Fore-* and the Latin Root *Vis-*
Working with Words with Multiple Meanings

Read the following historical **account** to learn how dogs came to be used as guides by people who have **visual** problems—handicaps related to their sight.

Morris Frank—A Visually Disabled Man with Vision

Morris Frank wondered if he would ever lead an independent life. **Accidentally** blinded in one eye when he was six years old and in the other eye when he was sixteen, Morris was **dependent** on companions to guide him wherever he went, even when he went on dates. He **yearned** to move about on his own. Personal **mobility** was something that he wanted and thought about more than anything else in life. He **envisioned** freedom to navigate on his own as part of his future.

The year 1927 was a **turning point** in Morris Frank's life. During that year, a significant event took place that would change him forever. One evening in November, Frank's father read a newspaper article to him explaining that the German government was training dogs to become guides for veterans who had been blinded during World War I. A **foresighted** man—one who could see ahead—Frank realized that a dog could be his **vehicle** to independence and mobility. He immediately wrote the author of the article, Dorothy Eustis, who was **breeding** German shepherds in Switzerland. Frank wrote, "Thousands of blind like me **abhor** being dependent on others. Help me and I will help them. Train me and I will bring back my dog and show people here how a blind man can be absolutely on his own."

Eustis could also **foresee** a time when blind people could get aroundby themselves with the help of only a guide dog. She invited Morris to come to Switzerland where she would train him to use a dog as his guide. In Switzerland, Morris Frank learned to handle Buddy, his first dog. This put Morris at the **forefront** of a movement to use seeing-eye dogs as guides for people with visual disabilities.

Returning to the United States, Morris Frank and Buddy traveled extensively. Frank demonstrated how useful Buddy was and created an outcry from other visually disabled people for dogs of their own. And so Frank opened The Seeing Eye in Memphis, Tennessee, in January of 1929. There he began to train guide dogs. In 1931, he moved the **enterprise**—the business—to Morristown, New Jersey, because it was too hot in Tennessee in the summer to train the dogs. Working at the Morristown site, Morris Frank became the **foremost** trainer of seeing-eye dogs in the United States.

Morris Frank died in 1980, but The Seeing Eye continues to this day as one of the leading guide dog schools in the country. If you go to Morristown, New Jersey, today and stand on a street corner downtown, you will see trainers walking the dogs. They are teaching the animals how to respond to commands and also to practice the art of intelligent disobedience. Intelligent disobedience is important because sometimes a blind person cannot **foretell** that there is a **hazard** along the path and commands the dog to move ahead. But the dog is trained to see the danger, ignore the command, and guide the owner to safety.

Seeing-eye dogs, however, play another significant role in the lives of their owners: They offer **companionship.** Often a guide dog becomes a blind person's best friend—a companion to go places with and even to talk to.

Thinking about Ideas and Relationships

1. What did Morris Frank hope to accomplish by getting a guide dog?

2. What do we mean when we say that seeing-eye dogs must use intelligent disobedience?

B Dealing with *Fore-* Words

The prefix *fore-* has been a part of the English language for a long time. *Fore-* means "in the front or before." If someone is in the forefront of the action, he or she is out front, a leader of the pack. Use your knowledge of the prefix *fore-* and context clues from the account on pages 50–51 to figure out the meanings of the highlighted words. Then complete the sentences based on your understanding of the *fore-* words.

1. If a person is **foresighted**, he or she ______________________________.
2. If a person is the **foremost** authority on a subject, he or she ______________________________.
3. If a person can **foresee** what is about to happen, he or she ______________________________.
4. The **forepaws** on a guide dog are the ones ______________________________.
5. The **foreword** of a book is found ______________________________.

C Dealing with the Latin Root *Vis-*

Complete each of the statements.

1. In Book 2 of *Words Are Wonderful*, you learned the words *visible* and *invisible*. If something is visible, you can see it. If something is invisible, you ______________________________.
2. The root *vis-* comes from a Latin word that means "to see" or "having sight." The word *visual* is formed from this root. Something that is visual is ______________________________.
3. People with good vision are those who ______________. People with poor vision are those who ______________________________.
4. Look up the word *envision* in your dictionary. A person who envisions a better world is one who ______________________________.
5. Morris Frank was a visually disabled man with vision because ______________________________.
6. Look up the word *visor* in your dictionary. A visor is a ______________________________.

Dealing with Words Built from the Latin Roots *Pend-/Pens-* and *Cid-/Cas-*

1. *Depend* is made up of two word elements: the Latin prefix *de-* (meaning "down") and the Latin root *pend-* (from a verb meaning "to hang"). When a person depends on a companion for assistance, he or she relies on, or places his or her faith in, a friend for help. The word tower below shows the kinship among *depend* and other words derived from the same root.

	de	pend	
	de	pend	ent
		pend	ing
		pend	ant
in	de	pend	ent
in	de	pend	ence

Explain how the words *dependent* and *independent* differ in meaning. Then write a sentence using both words.

2. The words *accident, accidental,* and *accidentally* are built from a Latin root (*cid-/cas-*) meaning "to fall or befall (happen)." When something happens accidentally, it happens by accident; it is something that just befalls, or happens to a person, for no apparent reason. In your notebook, write some sentences using the three words. Then make a short word tower, lining up the related parts of the three words to show their kinship.

Dealing with Multiple Meanings of Words

Read the two definitions of the word *vehicle* and the sentences that follow. Then fill in the circle that gives the definition of the word as used in the sentence.

vehicle (*noun*)

Definition 1. A device for carrying people or goods. (a literal use)

Definition 2. A means through which something is accomplished or achieved (a figurative use)

a. Frank realized that a dog could be his **vehicle** to independence.

① ②

b. The best **vehicle** for transporting your furniture is a van or truck.

① ②

Read the two definitions of the word *account* and the sentences that follow. Then fill in the circle that gives the definition of the word as used in the sentence.

account (*noun*)

Definition 1. An explanation; information on a topic given in sentence form, either orally or in writing.

Definition 2. A list or record of money received, spent, or owed.

a. I read a historical **account** about the building of the Suez Canal, a canal that connects the Mediterranean Sea with the Red Sea.

① ②

b. I kept an **account** of the money I earned during the summer.

① ②

Finding Definitions "Right There" in the Context of a Sentence or Paragraph

Find and record the synonym, definition, or explanation from the account about Morris Frank and The Seeing Eye on page 50 that gives you a good clue to the meaning of each word or expression below. The meanings are all "right there" in the account.

1. turning point: ______________________________
2. yearned: ______________________________
3. enterprise: ______________________________
4. companionship: ______________________________
5. hazard: ______________________________

In your notebook, write sentences with the five words or expressions that you have just defined.

G Guessing the Meanings of Words Based on Their Overall Context

Guess the meaning of each word by rereading the part of the selection where the word is found. Then write your guess in the table below. Next, replace the highlighted word in the sentence with your guess to see if it makes sense there. Finally, check your dictionary to see if your guess was correct. Add the dictionary definition and a sample sentence to the chart.

The Word	Your First Guess	The Dictionary Definition	A Sample Sentence
1. abhor			
2. mobility			
3. breeding			

STRATEGY CENTER

Use this strategy to decide the meaning of new words based on the overall sense of the sentence:

Guess the meaning of an unfamiliar word or expression based on its use in the sentence.

Check the dictionary.

Decide on the dictionary meaning that fits the context.

Reviewing Key Words

Write the letter of the definition on the line in front of the word.

Group One: Verbs

___ 1. yearn	a. to hate
___ 2. abhor	b. to see ahead into the future
___ 3. foresee	c. to picture in one's head
___ 4. envision	d. to tell what will happen in the future
___ 5. breed	e. to want more than anything else; to crave
___ 6. foretell	f. to raise, cultivate, or develop

Group Two: Adjectives

___ 7. dependent	g. outstanding; going beyond all others
___ 8. independent	h. relying on something or someone
___ 9. foresighted	i. not relying on something or someone; free
___ 10. accidental	j. related to sight
___ 11. visual	k. happening by accident; unplanned
___ 12. foremost	l. able to see ahead

Group Three: Nouns

___ 13. hazard	m. a written or oral explanation; a list of money received, spent, or owed
___ 14. companionship	n. a business
___ 15. mobility	o. friendship, especially companions doing things together
___ 16. account	p. a possible danger
___ 17. enterprise	q. sight
___ 18. visually	r. a means of achieving a purpose; a means of transportation
___ 19. vision	s. in a way that is related to sight
___ 20. vehicle	t. the ability to move

21. Use the phrase *turning point* in a sentence that clearly shows what a turning point is.

____

____

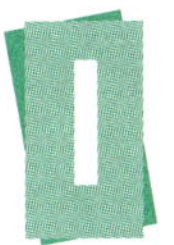

Writing Workshop

Great leaders should have a vision. They should be able to envision a better future and be able to help others achieve higher goals. One leader who had a vision for his country was Abraham Lincoln. Write an account explaining Lincoln's contribution to the United States. You might want to write about the Emancipation Proclamation, through which Lincoln tried to ensure that his vision would come true, as well as the Gettysburg Address. Search the Web for information to include in your account. Be sure to use quotation marks when you use another person's words and footnotes to credit your sources.

The Latin Roots Press- and Spec-/Spic-/Spect- and Review of the Latin Prefixes Re- and Con-/Com-/Col-/Co-

Reviewing Acronyms

In Lesson 4, you learned that elephants live in families and have feelings toward one another. Listen as your teacher reads aloud the following account about dolphins. Keep asking, "What evidence do we have that dolphins are intelligent? How are dolphins similar to elephants? How are they different?"

Are Dolphins as Intelligent as Human Beings?

Recently, Gae Savino and her children took a trip to Florida and swam with the dolphins. As she later **recounted,** "We got right into the water with these **impressive** creatures. We were able to observe, touch, and play with them. As we were inspecting them, they returned our **inspection,** looking us over from head to toe. They watched what we were doing and then amazingly they **mimicked** our actions. They did exactly what we did. We had the opportunity to feed them, and my teenage daughter had the opportunity to train them—to get them to do what she wanted them to. It was awesome!"[1]

Dolphins are **spectacular** animals. They are sea mammals, closely akin to whales. A little smaller than whales, adult dolphins are about 8 feet long and weigh about 165 pounds. They are absolutely beautiful when they leap gracefully out of the water; they **arch** their bodies—snout down, back curved up, tail fins down. They seem to smile all the time—a **feature,** or characteristic, that is a result of the shape of their mouth and the position of their teeth.

Dolphins can swim very fast. They have been observed swimming thirty miles per hour when they are **pressed**—when they are under some kind of pressure, or strain. Their average speed, however, is about twenty-four miles per hour. Dolphins have also been observed **hitching** a ride on the bow of a ship and even on the front of a whale. What a fantastic **spectacle!**

1. Gae Savino in a personal communication with the author.

But the most outstanding feature of dolphins is their ability to **converse** with one another and work together as a group. The dolphins use a system of whistles, clicks, and squeaks to "talk" to one another. Biologists believe that this system is complex, and they have collected **considerable** evidence to support that conclusion. Here is an example of that evidence.

As part of a study of animal behavior, scientists Dr. John Dreher and Dr. William E. Evans of California Lockhead Company stuck some aluminum poles upright at the entrance, or opening, to a lagoon. On the poles they mounted microphones to pick up underwater sounds. The result was a **barrier** that made access to the lagoon appear difficult. By chance, five bottle-nosed dolphins showed up a short distance from the barrier. From **afar,** they studied the barrier and began to converse with one another. The microphones picked up their clicks, squeaks, and whistles—their conversation. The dolphins looked as though they were deciding whether it was safe to enter the lagoon. They looked as though they were hatching a plan to deal with the possible hazard.

Then, one dolphin—a **scout**—left the group and began a closer examination of the poles. The microphones picked up sounds that the scout was sending out—what are called **sonar** soundings. The scout could hear the echoes of the sounds it was sending out. It used those echoes to figure out the size, shape, and location of the poles. *Sonar* is an acronym that stands for *so*und *na*vigation *r*anging. Submarines use a similar sonar system to navigate—to find their way in the water.

Having **inspected** the situation, the dolphin scout returned to its group—its **pod**—to give its report. At that point, the microphones picked up the clicks, squeaks, and whistles the dolphins made as they "talked" together. After they had conversed for a time, the pod of dolphins crossed the barrier into the lagoon. Interestingly, when the dolphins were ready to leave the lagoon, they swam out without **reexamining** the barrier. They "knew" that there was no danger. They seemed to have remembered.

This cooperative, problem-solving behavior has made people ask, "Are dolphins as intelligent as we are?" The question is hard to answer. We know that dolphins make and use tools. They tease other creatures and play **pranks** on them. Dolphins also live together in social groups and take turns babysitting their young. They get **depressed** when they are alone for a long time.

We know, too, that dolphins can be trained. You can see them being trained if you visit an environmental education center where dolphins perform. You will see dolphins responding to a variety of commands and cooperating with their trainers. You will come away with respect for these marvelous mammals and with the clear impression that dolphins are intelligent creatures. You may decide you want to be more than a **spectator**—and that you too would love to swim with the dolphins as Gae Savino and her family did.

Thinking about Ideas and Relationships

1. What evidence do we have to indicate that dolphins are intelligent?

2. How are dolphins similar to elephants? How are they different? Complete the Venn diagram using information from the accounts given in Lessons 4 and 8 as well as any other information you may recall.

Features Unique to Dolphins | **Features Shared by Dolphins and Elephants** | **Features Unique to Elephants**

B Dealing with the Latin Root *Press-*

The Latin root *press-* means "to press, or to exert a force on." You find this root in five words in the account about dolphins: *impressive, pressed, pressure, depressed,* and *impression.* You may have heard or read other words that belong to this large word family: *press, pressing, repress, repression, repressive, compress, compression, express,* and *expression.* Based on the meaning of the root and context clues, complete the following sentences. You may also use a dictionary to check your hypotheses.

1. When you **press** your clothes, you ______________________________
____.

2. When you are being **pressed** to do something, you ______________________
____.

3. When someone puts **pressure** on you to participate, they ____________________

____.

4. An **impressive** animal is one that ___________________________________

____.

5. When you get an **impression** about something, you ________________________

____.

6. When you are **depressed,** you _______________________________________

____.

C Dealing with the Latin Root *Spec-/Spic-/Spect-*

The Latin root *spec-/spic-/spect-* means "to look." You find this root in six words in the account about dolphins: *inspect, inspection, spectacular, spectacle, spectator,* and *respect.* Other related words are *spectacles, specimen, spectrum, specter, speculate, introspection, retrospection,* and *respectable.* This, too, is a large word family. Based on the meaning of the root and context clues, answer the following questions. You may also use a dictionary to check your hypotheses.

1. What do you do when you **inspect** something?

2. What do you do when you make an **inspection**?

3. Dolphins are **spectacular** animals. What do we mean when we say that?

4. "What a **spectacle!**" my friend exclaimed when she saw the circus acrobats. What did the friend mean when she said that? What is a spectacle?

5. What does a **spectator** do?

6. If you **respect** dolphins, how do you feel about them?

D Reviewing the Prefix *Re-*

You may recall that the prefix *re-* means "again or backward." You find *re-* on these words from the account about dolphins: *reexamined, recount, report, remember,* and *respect.* Based on the meaning of *re-* and context clues from the selection, match the words with their definitions by writing the letter of the definition on the line in front of the correct word.

___ 1. reexamine	a. to think highly of
___ 2. recount	b. to look over once again
___ 3. report	c. to recall
___ 4. remember	d. to tell a story about
___ 5. respect	e. to give the details of

Make a web of *re-* words in your notebook. Start by writing the prefix at the center of the web. List examples extending outward from the center. Use your dictionary to find other words with *re-*. Include in your web only words you can define.

Reviewing *Con-/Com-/Col-/Co-* Words

The prefix *con-/com-/col-/co-* means "together." You find this prefix on these words from the selection about dolphins: *converse, conversation, considerable, conclusion, communication, complex, collected,* and *cooperating.* Based on the meaning of *con-/com-/col-/co-*, context clues from the selection, and what you remember from studying the prefix in Book 3 of *Words Are Wonderful,* match the words with their definitions. Write the letter of the definition on the line in front of the correct word.

___ 1. converse	a. the act of talking together
___ 2. collect	b. having two or more parts; involved; complicated
___ 3. communication	c. to pull ideas together in a report; to reach a decision; to end
___ 4. complex	d. to gather together
___ 5. conclude	e. to talk together
___ 6. considerable	f. to work together with others
___ 7. cooperate	g. large in amount; lots of

Make a word tower in your notebook that highlights the kinship among the words on page 62. Add to your tower other *con-/com-/col-/co-* words that you find in the dictionary or can remember. Include only words you can define.

F Using Context and Dictionary Clues to Define New Words

Give the meaning of each of these words by finishing the sentences. You can take phrases right from the selection to use in your definitions or look up the meanings in a dictionary. Remember to list the meaning that is correct in the context of the selection.

1. If you **mimic** someone's actions, you ____________________.
2. If you **arch** your body, you ____________________.
3. If you **hitch** a ride, you ____________________.
4. A **feature** of something is a ____________________.
5. A **barrier** is something that ____________________.
6. If you **press** someone to do something, you ____________________.
7. A **pod** of whales is ____________________.
8. **Sonar** uses echoes as a means of ____________________.
9. If you play a **prank** on someone, you ____________________.
10. If you observe something from **afar**, you ____________________.
11. If you **recount** a story, you ____________________.
12. If you make a good **impression** on someone, you ____________________ ____________________.

Reviewing New Words by Dealing with Context Clues

Here are two paragraphs that paraphrase (or recount in a different way) the information about dolphins on pages 58–59. In each case, select the word that best fits in each blank.

Group One

afar arch converse mimic pods pranks sonar spectacular spectator

Dolphins live together in groups called ____________________. They "talk," or ____________________, with one another through a system of clicks and whistles, and they navigate using ________________. They ________________ the actions of other animals; if you flip onto your back while swimming, they will do that too. If you ____________ your back as you swim, they too will curve the middle of their backs upward. And they love to tease and play ____________ on other animals. Dolphins are really ____________________ creatures—unique in so many different ways. It's great to be a ________________ at a performance of dolphins at an environmental center. It's fantastic to view these mammals close-up rather than from ________________.

Group Two

barrier considerable reexamining impressive inspect inspection scout

Biologists are ____________________ their conclusions about animal intelligence based on the ____________________ behavior of dolphins. For example, members of a pod will send out a ________________ to decide whether a situation is dangerous. The dolphin that is sent out will carefully ______________ something that seems to be a hazard. For example, if there is a __________________ that sits across the entrance to a lagoon, the scout will look it over. After making its ____________________, the scout will return to the pod to give a report. The returning scout makes a ____________________ amount of noise, clicking and whistling to communicate its message.

Make up your own sentences using these words. You can look back to the selection and model your sentences after those found there. For the word *hitch*, check the dictionary for a second meaning and write a second sentence with that meaning.

1. depressed

2. feature (noun)

3. press (don't use it in the context of ironing clothes)

4. recount

5. spectacle

6. hitch

Writing Workshop

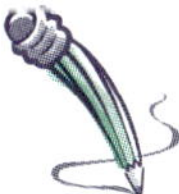

The opening paragraph is a very important part of an account. Notice that the account about the dolphins starts by recounting the adventures of the Savino family rather than giving considerable detail about dolphins. The author wrote her introduction in that way to "hook" her readers. Consider writing an account about another intelligent animal such as a chimpanzee or a gorilla. Start by recounting an interesting event that will make your reader want to continue. Get your information from the Internet or from a trade book in your library.

The Latin Roots Serve- and Cred- and the Prefix En-/Em-

Distinguishing Shades of Meaning

The word *cause* has several meanings. In some contexts, *cause* means "to make happen" or "what makes something happen." In other contexts, a *cause* relates to "a movement that people believe in, join, or support," such as the cause of freedom. Read to find out how African Americans helped the American **cause** during the Revolutionary War. Also, as you read, think about this question: What is the difference between an illegal and an immoral act?

Up from Bondage—The Military Road to Freedom

Today, in the United States military **service** is voluntary. Some young people choose to **enlist** after they graduate from high school or college. In the past also, some men and women signed up voluntarily, of their own free will. For example, during the Second World War, Presidents John Fitzgerald Kennedy, Lyndon Baines Johnson, and George Herbert Walker Bush enlisted and served in the navy.

At times, military service has been required. During the American Revolution, some men were **drafted,** or pulled into, the Continental Army and told they must serve. At that time, it was legal for a man to hire a **substitute** to take his place. Under the law, men could **engage,** or employ, others to fulfill their responsibilities. They could even ask their servants to take their places in the army. Slave owners also had the choice of sending their slaves—who were in servitude to them—instead of fulfilling their military duty themselves.

In the mid-1700s, Samuel Sutphen was a slave—not on a plantation in the far South but on a farm in New Jersey. Sutphen's owner promised him freedom if he would take his place in what was called "the militia." Samuel Sutphen later wrote, "I believed the white man's word, hoping to be free when the fight was over. I took no paper to show the bargain, but trusted to my master."[1]

Sutphen's tour of duty lasted three months, but when he returned home, his master **reneged** on his promise. Instead of freeing the man

1. William Gordon, "Soldiering for Freedom: Blacks, Slaves, and Freedmen Were Part of the Fight for American Independencce," *The Star-Ledger,* Friday, February 20. 2004, pp. 61–62.

who had taken his place in the front lines as he had promised, Sutphen's master sold him to another slaveholder! **Incredibly,** this second master also sent Sutphen to substitute for him in the militia.

Samuel Sutphen survived his second tour of duty only to be sold to a third master. This master was a little fairer. He encouraged Samuel to work off his sale price. When Samuel did, he released Samuel from **bondage**—from slavery. The master's name was Sutphen, and so Samuel took that as his **surname** when he was freed.

Years later, Samuel Sutphen **applied** for a **pension,** money paid to him based on his **credentials** as a veteran who had fought in the Revolutionary War. After Sutphen sent in his application, he was told that he would not get what he had earned and **deserved.** His first master had been **credited** for Samuel's tours of duty. Sutphen's application was rejected because no one could find a record saying he had served. At that point, Sutphen got nothing. Only after Sutphen had sent in his records many times did he finally receive a yearly pension of fifty dollars. He got that annual payment until he died at age 94 in 1841.

Samuel Sutphen was not the only African American to serve in the Continental Army during the American Revolution. Oliver Cromwell, a freeman, enlisted willingly—voluntarily. He crossed the Delaware River with Washington and fought with courage in many battles. Another black freeman, Cyrus Bustill, **wintered** with George Washington at the Valley Forge **encampment.** He spent the winter at the camp and put up with almost unbearable conditions there.

Of his own free will, Jack Banquante, a slave, volunteered his services as a substitute for his master. He fought bravely in many battles and was freed by his master when he returned home. A slave named Prime escaped from his master and enlisted in the Continental Army. He fought courageously, and after the war was over, was given his freedom by his state legislature. All these and many, many other African Americans **endured** incredible hardships on the battlefield. In **recognition** of their contribution to the Revolutionary War, Emmanuel Leutze, who painted a famous picture of George Washington crossing the Delaware, placed a black soldier just in front of General Washington in the boat. Leutze did this to give **credit** to all the African Americans—slaves and free black men alike—who saw service during the American Revolution.

These men **embraced** the American **cause** of winning freedom and independence from Great Britain. Sadly, although the Declaration of Independence stated that "all men are created equal," at the end of the war the United States adopted a constitution that permitted people to keep others in bondage. It allowed people to keep others as slaves. This **immoral** practice—a practice that is against everything that is right and good—continued to be legal in America. Slavery became illegal in America only with the **enactment,** or passage, of the Thirteenth Amendment to the United States Constitution in 1865.

Thinking about Ideas and Relationships

1. What was the American cause and how did African Americans contribute to that cause during the Revolutionary War? Use the word *cause* in your answer.

2. To hold someone in bondage was immoral even when slavery was legal in the United States. Explain the difference between something that is legal and something that is moral, and between something that is illegal and something that is immoral.

Recognizing the Latin Root *Serv-*

The Latin root *serv-* means "to serve or to save." On pages 66–67, you can find *serv-* in the English words *serve, service, servant, servitude,* and *deserve.* You may remember seeing it in the words *conserve, conservation, reserve, reservation, preserve,* and *preservation.* Complete these sentences in the spaces provided. Use the meaning of the root to guide you.

1. When a person gives **service** in the armed forces, he or she ______________________

   ____.

2. A **servant** is a person who ____.

3. If a person **deserves** a pension, he or she __________________________________.

4. A person who is held in **servitude** is ____________________________________.

5. To **preserve** the environment means ____________________________________.

Recognizing the Latin Root *Cred-*

1. The Latin root *cred-* means "to believe or to trust." On pages 66–67, you can find this root in the English words *credit* (used as both a noun and a verb), *incredibly,* and *credentials.* You may also remember seeing it in the words *creditor, creed, credible, incredible, accredit,* and *discredit.* Complete the following word tree by writing the word meanings next to the words on the branches. You can use the dictionary to define the words and perhaps find other *cred-* words to hang on the tree. You will find that the word *credit* has multiple meanings, so include several definitions on your tree.

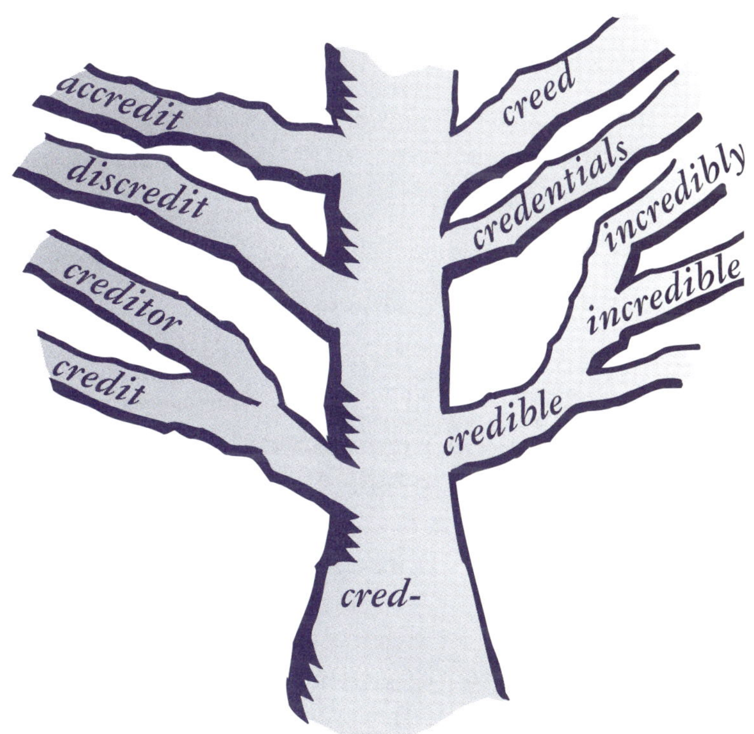

2. Write the letter of the definition on the line in front of the correct word.

____ incredible	a. evidence that one has a right to receive something; a written record that shows what one has done
____ credible	b. not believable
____ credit (noun)	c. to give official recognition to
____ credit (verb)	d. recognition
____ credentials	e. believable

D Reviewing the Prefix *En-/Em-*

En-/em- means "in or into." When a person is **enslaved,** he or she is forced into bondage—forced to become a slave. You can see the word *slave* right there in the word *enslaved.* You can also see the prefix *en-* at the beginning of the word.

1. Circle the prefix on the highlighted words in the sentences below. Underline the shorter base word or root that you recognize within the longer word. Then answer the questions based on the way the highlighted words are used in the selection and the elements you can see "right there" in each word.

   a. What does a person do when he or she **encourages** someone to **enlist** as a volunteer in the Peace Corps?

   b. What is an **encampment**?

   c. What does Congress do when it **enacts** laws?

2. When you strip the prefix *en-/em-* from the words *engage, embrace,* and *endure,* you may not recognize the base word or root. You can figure out the meanings, however, from context clues. Go back and find the words on pages 66–67. Then match the words with their definitions and write the letter of each definition on the line in front of the correct word.

   ___ to engage — a. to hire or employ

   ___ to embrace — b. to carry on, despite great hardships; to put up with hardships

   ___ to endure — c. to take on a cause eagerly and willingly

3. The word *embrace* has another, more literal, meaning. If one person embraces another person, what does he or she do?

Getting More Assistance from Context Clues

Write down the words or phrases from the article on pages 66–67 that are clues to the meaning of these nouns and verbs.

1. a pension: (noun) ______
2. to renege: (verb) ______
3. a cause: (noun) ______
4. to cause: (verb) ______
5. surname: (noun) ______
6. bondage: (noun) ______
7. to be drafted: (verb) ______
8. a substitute: (noun) ______
9. to substitute for: (verb) ______
10. to winter: (verb) ______
11. to apply: (verb) ______
12. recognition: (noun) ______
13. enactment: (noun) ______

Reviewing the Highlighted Words

Paraphrase the following statements by restating them without using the highlighted words. You may use another form of a highlighted word—for example, *serve* rather than *service, recognition* rather than *recognize.*

1. My grandparents **wintered** in Florida.

2. When I lived in Florida, Grandma and Grandpa Malla always **drafted me** to drive them into the city.

3. I was glad to be of **service** to my grandparents.

4. Now that I've moved away, my grandparents have **engaged** someone else when they want to go into town.

5. My grandparents' **surname** is Malla.

6. Because Grandpa is a **veteran,** he **applied** for a **pension** that he **deserved.**

7. My brother Hal **reneged** on his pledge to **enlist** his friends in a paper-recycling program at school.

8. My sister Flo has **incredible endurance**; she swims more than two miles every day.

9. With the **enactment** of the Thirteenth Amendment, **bondage** became **illegal** in the United States.

10. When Vinny **embraces** a **cause**, he works **incredibly** hard.

11. Vinny **endures** a lot even though his family does not **encourage** him or **recognize** how hard he works.

12. Gea asked me to **substitute** for her in the final race but I told her this was not permitted.

13. Tia has very impressive **credentials**, but she always **credits** those who have contributed to her success.

14. Tia is a very **moral** person; in contrast, Gea has acted in ways I consider immoral.

Writing Workshop

To renege on a pledge is immoral, although in some instances it may be legal. You may want to write about a time when someone reneged on a promise to you. In your account, tell what happened and how you felt.

At some point, you may want to write about a cause in which you believe strongly. In your report, explain what the cause is and why you feel strongly about it. Also ask others their opinions and include those opinions as quotations in your paper.

Consider taking time to read the features section of your regional newspaper. Often you will find articles on very interesting topics. Use facts from an article that you enjoy as the jumping-off point for a report that you write. Note that both this selection and the selection in Lesson 2 are based on facts from featured articles in a regional newspaper.

The Elements *Tele-*, *Phon-*, *Gram-*/*Graph-*, and *Omni-*; and the Suffix *-Ular*/*-Ar*

Mining the Dictionary

Listen to the following explanation to learn how cell phones work and why *cellular telephone* is a good phrase to describe this technological device. Some of the words in the selection are long and complex and are derived from Latin and Greek roots.

Wireless Communication—Waves Are What It Is All About

Stand on any street corner in many parts of the world and you will see people walking along and **simultaneously** talking on cell phones to friends who are miles away. You can observe this same **phenomenon**—this same remarkable thing—in parks, schoolyards, supermarkets, and restaurants. The use of cell phones is **ubiquitous.** Because they are found all over, you can't escape these devices, which are **omnipresent,** or present wherever you go.

Cell phone is a shortened, or clipped, form of the phrase *cellular telephone.* This phrase tells you a lot about this gadget, a device invented so recently that its name is not listed in older dictionaries. The word *cellular* has two elements: *cell,* from a Latin word meaning "chamber," and the suffix *-ular,* meaning "resembling." *Cellular* means "relating to or resembling a cell or box-like structure." The word *telephone* also has two elements: *tele-,* meaning "far," and *phone-,* meaning "sound or voice." Both *tele-* and *phone-* are derived from Greek. A telephone is an instrument for sending sound across distances. Keep reading to learn why *cellular telephone* is a wonderful phrase for a device that is so ubiquitous that you find people using these phones wherever you go.

How does a cell phone work? Before the days of wireless **telecommunication,** telephone messages were sent over wires. Wires connected one phone to another. For example, if you lived in Oregon and you **phoned** someone in South Carolina, your message was sent from wire to wire until it reached the person you had dialed. In those days, too, there was literally a dial rather than a keypad on the phone. It was a **rotary** dial that rotated, or turned around, as you dialed the number of the person you wanted to reach.

Today, telecommunication systems are extremely complex. When you speak into the **microphone** of a cell phone, the internal circuit board converts the sounds of your voice into electrical waves that the phone sends, or **radiates,** outward. Those waves are invisible, but they exist nonetheless. The electrical waves are picked up by a cell-phone tower, which sends the waves onward to another tower. That tower **relays,** or passes the waves on, to still another tower, **et cetera** and et cetera. Eventually the waves that make up your message reach a central station. In turn, the station passes the waves of your message from tower to tower until they reach the cell phone of the person whose number you dialed. Your phone also sends a special code as part of the message so that your cell-phone provider can charge you for your call.

To make this wireless system work, the country has been divided into small cells, or units. (Now you know why your phone is called a *cellular phone*!) Each cell is about 10 square miles and on each one is a cell-phone tower. If you drive along most major highways, you will see cell-phone towers. Note the **graphic** on page 74.

A cell-phone tower is a tall metal pole with lots of metal **antennae** sticking outward. Some of the **telecom** companies have tried to **disguise** their towers. They attempt to make the towers look like trees by affixing green, branch-like metal pieces. Unfortunately, the resulting structures do not usually **deceive,** or fool, anyone.

There are a few things you should know if you want to be an effective cell phone user. First, don't get your cell phone wet. Water can **corrode,** or eat away, the inner workings of the device. If your phone accidentally gets wet, don't turn it on until it has dried out.

Second, don't leave your phone in a hot place. Extreme heat can affect the battery in a negative way. The same is true of cold, so don't let your phone get **unduly** cold.

Third, be polite when you use your phone so that you don't become a public **nuisance,** someone who bothers other people. Don't speak so loudly that you disturb people close by. Turn off your phone when you are in public places such as theatres, restaurants, and classrooms. Other people do not want to be bothered when your phone rings or if you get up to take a call. When used wisely, however, a cell phone is a wonderful means of communication.

Thinking about Ideas and Relationships

1. Why is *cellular telephone* a good name for a wireless phone?

2. How does a cell phone work?

Mining the Dictionary for Complex Words with Latin and Greek Origins

1. Reread the first paragraph of the selection on page 74 and think about the meaning of the word *simultaneously*.

   a. What context clues do you see that hint at the meaning of *simultaneously?*

   b. *Simultaneously* begins with the root *simul-,* meaning "the same." Can you think of any other words that use this root? If you can, write them here.

   c. What do you think *simultaneously* means?

   d. What is the dictionary definition of *simultaneously*?

STRATEGY CENTER

Use this step-by-step strategy for dealing with a complex word:

1. Study the context for any clues to meaning.
2. Look for any affixes, roots, or base words that you recognize in the complex word.
3. Hypothesize the meaning of the new word based on context clues and word elements you recognize.
4. Study the multiple meanings of the word that the dictionary provides to see if your hypothesis is on target.
5. Decide which meaning works in the sentence you are trying to understand.

2. Reread the first paragraph of the selection and think about the meaning of *phenomenon.*

   a. What is the meaning of *phenomenon* based on context clues that are right there in the sentence?

   b. What is the main dictionary definition of *phenomenon*?

   c. What is the origin of the word *phenomenon*?

   d. What does your dictionary give as the plural of *phenomenon*?

   e. Be ready to pronounce *phenomenon*, based on the diacritical marks shown in the dictionary entry.

3. Reread the last two sentences of the first paragraph.

   a. Based on context clues, hypothesize the meanings of *ubiquitous* and *omnipresent.*

   b. Look up *ubiquitous* in the dictionary. Note how to pronounce it. What is the meaning of *ubiquitous* according to the dictionary?

   c. What is the origin of the word *ubiquitous*?

   d. Check *omnipresent* in the dictionary. Note how to pronounce it. What is the meaning of *omnipresent* according to the dictionary?

   e. What is the origin of the word *omnipresent?*

   f. What is the meaning of the prefix *omni-*, according to your dictionary?

   g. In the dictionary, find two other words that start with the prefix *omni-*. Write the three words as a word tower to highlight the kinship among the words.

omni present

   h. Are *ubiquitous* and *omnipresent* synonyms, antonyms, or homonyms? Write your answer here.

4. Before the days of wireless telecommunication, telephone messages were sent over wires.

   a. What is the meaning of the root *tele-* in the word *telecommunication*? Check your dictionary and write the definition here.

b. What other word in sentence 4 is a clue to the meaning of *communication*?

c. What is the meaning of *telecommunication*? After you have written your definition based on context clues and word elements, check your hypothesis in the dictionary and rewrite your definition here.

d. Note the word *telecom* later in the article. What do you think *telecom* stands for?

5. You read that electrical waves are picked up by a cell-phone tower, which sends the waves on to another tower. The second tower relays them, or passes them on, to still another tower, et cetera and et cetera.

   a. Based on the context, guess what *et cetera* means? Write your guess here, check your definition in the dictionary, and then revise your definition based on what the dictionary says.

   b. Guess what the abbreviation *etc.* stands for?

   c. Based on the context, guess the meaning of *relay.* The meaning is given "right there" in the sentence so that you don't have to use a dictionary unless you wish to. Write the definition here.

6. A cell-phone tower is a tall metal pole with metal antennae sticking outward.

   a. Check the pronunciation and meaning of *antennae* in your dictionary. What two main meanings do you find? Write the two here and circle the one that relates to the word's use in sentence 6.

   b. What is the singular form of *antennae*, according to your dictionary?

7. The word *phone* can function as either a noun or verb.

   a. Write a sentence using *phone* as a verb.

   b. Check the section of your dictionary that contains the word *phone.* In that section, locate two other words that are built from the root *phon-*. List them here with their definitions.

8. Check the word *microphone* in your dictionary.

   a. What does *micro-* mean? (Check the etymology part of the entry for *microphone.*)

   b. What is a microphone?

9. Look up the root *graph-* in your dictionary.

   a. What is the meaning of the root?

   b. What is its origin?

   c. Hypothesize the meaning of *graphic* based on your knowledge of the root *graph-* and the way the word is used in the selection. Write your hypothesis here.

   d. What meanings does your dictionary give for the word *graphic*? Write at least two.

   e. Check your hypothesis. Were you correct about the meaning of *graphic* as used in the selection? If not, write the meaning here that relates to its use in the selection.

C Relying on Context Clues

Study the way the following words are used in the selection to decide on their meaning. Find the best definition for each word and write the letter of the definition on the line in front of the word. Then write a sentence that uses the word in the space beneath each item.

____ 1. rotary | a. to make something or someone look different, usually to deceive

____ 2. radiate | b. turning round and round

____ 3. disguise | c. a bother; something that upsets or disturbs

____ 4. deceive | d. to eat away, as iron is eaten away by rust

____ 5. corrode | e. extremely; far more than usual

____ 6. unduly | f. to send outward, especially to send energy waves outward

____ 7. nuisance | g. to fool or trick

Reviewing the Highlighted Words

Complete the crossword puzzles using these words:

antennae corrode deceive disguise etc. graphic microphone nuisance omnipresent phenomenon phone radiate rotary relay simultaneously telecom telecommunication ubiquitous unduly

CLUES

Across

4. visual display
5. abbreviation for *et cetera*
8. at the same time
9. turning round and round
10. call on the telephone

Down

1. being, or seeming to be, everywhere at the same time
2. make something look different so as to deceive
3. eat away, as iron is eaten away by rust
6. clipped word for *telecommunication*
7. send outward, as to send sound energy outward

Complete the crossword puzzles using these words:

antennae corrode deceive disguise etc. graphic microphone nuisance omnipresent phenomenon phone radiate rotary relay simultaneously telecom telecommunication ubiquitous unduly

CLUES

Across

4. electrical message sent via telephone, television, radio, etc.
6. a pest; something that is bothersome
8. far more than usual; extremely
9. fool or trick

Down

1. present everywhere
2. an observable fact or event; a remarkable thing
3. metal prongs used to receive television signals
5. an electronic gadget you talk into
7. passing something along from one to another

Writing Workshop

During Writing Workshop, go online or check library trade books for information about another technological advance such as the computer and email, television, or the supersonic jet. Write a brief explanation telling how the device or machine works.

Similes and Metaphors, the Prefix Be-, and the Suffix -Ful

Distinguishing Fact from Fiction

As you listen to the following Greek myth, ask yourself why the ancient Greeks devised **fanciful** tales like this one about Arachne and Athena.

Arachne and Athena—A Clash of Egos

Arachne was a young maiden who lived in a **remote** village in Greece, far from the great cities of Athens and Sparta. Although she lived in an out-of-the-way place, Arachne was known all over Greece for her ability to spin thread and weave cloth. With the strands of brilliantly colored wool that she made on her spinning wheel, Arachne wove woolen cloth that was magnificent to **behold**. People came from far and wide to see the cloth and watch Arachne's fingers crisscrossing her loom. Arachne's fingers flashed back and forth like lightning across the summer sky.

One day, a man who was watching Arachne weaving with woolen thread as fine as a hair exclaimed to a friend, "Athena, the goddess of wisdom, must have taught Arachne how to spin and weave. How else could she weave **fabric** that looks like a field of wildflowers in the sunshine?"

Arachne heard the comment and was **peeved**—really annoyed and uptight. Praise had raised her **ego** to such a great height that she now thought of herself as an even better weaver than the goddess Athena. She turned to the man and exploded, "Don't credit Athena for teaching me my craft. After all, my woolen cloth is more beautiful and colorful than anything that Athena can weave. I take complete credit. I am the better weaver. I challenge Athena to come down from her home on Mt. Olympus. I will show her that I am better than the **immortal** gods—those beings that never die and live forever and ever."

As it turned out, Athena was nearby and heard Arachne's challenge. She quickly changed her appearance and stood before Arachne in the **guise** of a poorly dressed, old woman. Disguised in this shabby way, the goddess **berated** Arachne. She scolded her by saying, "Apologize for your **disrespectful** words. Be satisfied to be the best weaver among **mortal** beings. Do not **besmirch** the gods of Mt. Olympus. Do not stain their reputations. If you continue to **belittle** the gods, a terrible fate will **befall** you."

These words angered Arachne even more. "I **resent** what you are saying, old woman," she replied. Hearing Arachne's disrespectful answer, the old woman began to grow taller and taller. The **bedraggled** clothes she was wearing turned into sparkling white robes. Everyone realized that this was the all-powerful Athena, the goddess who had **bestowed** her name on the city of Athens.

Athena sat down immediately at a loom in Arachne's workroom. She began to weave a magnificent, heavy piece of cloth, a **tapestry** with a colorful, picture-like scene. Those who watched saw that Athena was weaving a picture that communicated a final warning to Arachne to take back her **egocentric** words.

That did not stop Arachne. She sat down at her loom and began to weave a tapestry with designs that belittled Athena and the other mighty gods and goddesses of Mt. Olympus.

When Athena saw what Arachne had done, she looked at her challenger with eyes that blazed like the sun on a hot day. "You have besmirched me and the other gods and goddesses. I will punish you for your insults. In the future, people will look at you and your descendants with **repugnance**. People will look upon you in total disgust."

With that, Athena turned her angry eyes upon Arachne, and Arachne began to **shrivel** up. Her body got smaller and drier; her legs grew short and crooked. Three more pairs of legs sprang into place on her body, which became furry. There, before everyone's eyes, Arachne took on a different form—the form of a spider. And, to this day, according to the Greek myth, all the descendants of Arachne—her children and her children's children—continue to spin their webs day in and day out.

So the next time you see a spider, recall the myth about Arachne and Athena. But recall, too, the scientific facts about spiders. Spiders belong to the phylum Arthropoda, class Arachnida, order Aranae. They have four pairs of legs, a two-part body, and three pairs of spinnerets. The spinnerets are tube-like structures from which spiders secrete the fine threads with which they build their webs. Spider webs are delicate traps. In these traps, spiders catch unsuspecting prey—insects that they eat for food.

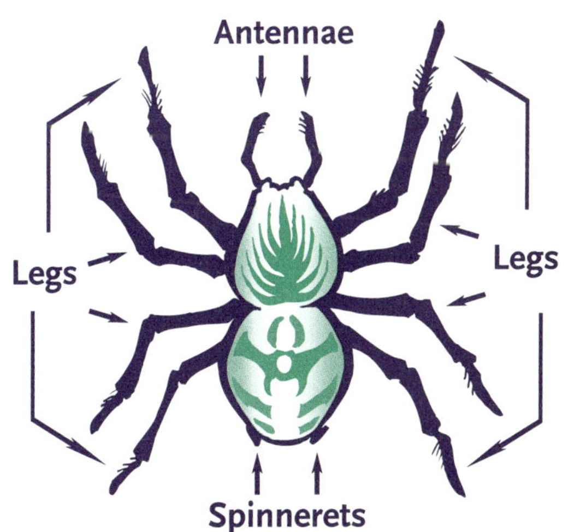

Are the facts about spiders more interesting than the Greek myth? That's for you to decide. Just remember that myths and scientific facts serve different purposes. Myths are stepping stones into the world of the imagination. Facts are bridges into the world of scientific knowledge.

Thinking about Ideas and Relationships

1. Why do you think the ancient Greeks devised fanciful tales such as the one about Arachne and Athena?

2. What can happen when egos clash?

3. "Pride goeth before a fall" is an old proverb, or maxim. How does the saying relate to the story of Arachne and Athena?

Going on a Word Scavenger Hunt

In a scavenger hunt, players must locate a series of items. In a word scavenger hunt, players must find words that have been defined. Here are the definitions of some words highlighted in the myth on pages 84–85. Search the myth for the highlighted word that best fits each definition. Write the word on the line.

1. really annoyed; uptight: ______________________
2. far off the beaten track; out of the way: ______________________
3. disgust or extreme dislike: ______________________
4. woven cloth: ______________________
5. a magnificent, heavy piece of woven cloth that contains picture-like scenes: ________
6. without respect; rude ______________________
7. the self; the inner part of oneself: ______________________
8. focused on the self; self-centered: ______________________
9. unreal; full of fantastic things: ______________________
10. lasting forever; not having to die: ______________________
11. not lasting forever, must die: ______________________

12. outward look or appearance, sometimes false; a way of dressing: ______________

13. to feel bitter, to be filled with ill will: ______________

14. to get smaller in size and dry out: ______________

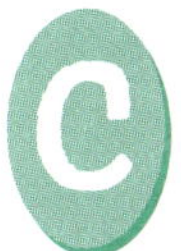

Interpreting the Meanings of Figures of Speech

As you learned in Book 3 of *Words Are Wonderful*, a *simile* is a creative comparison in which a writer or speaker says that one thing is like a second thing. He or she transfers ideas we usually connect with one object to a second object that is very different. To make the comparison, an author or speaker uses the words *like* or *as*. An example of a simile is "The virus spread like wildfire."

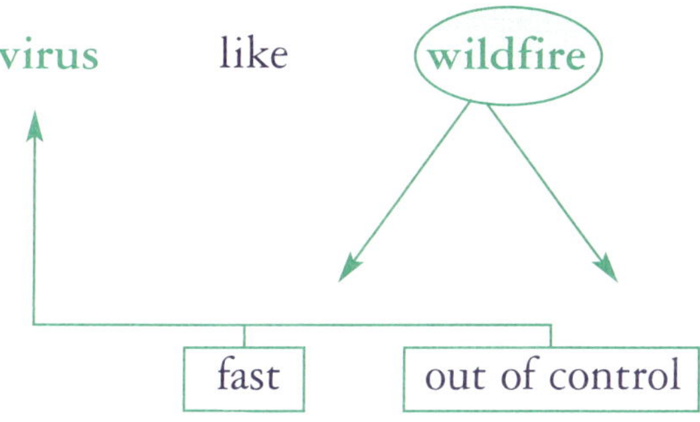

This simile makes us realize that the virus spreads fast and is out of control.

A *metaphor* is a creative comparison in which an author relates two different things without using *like* or *as*. An example is "Life is an elevator."

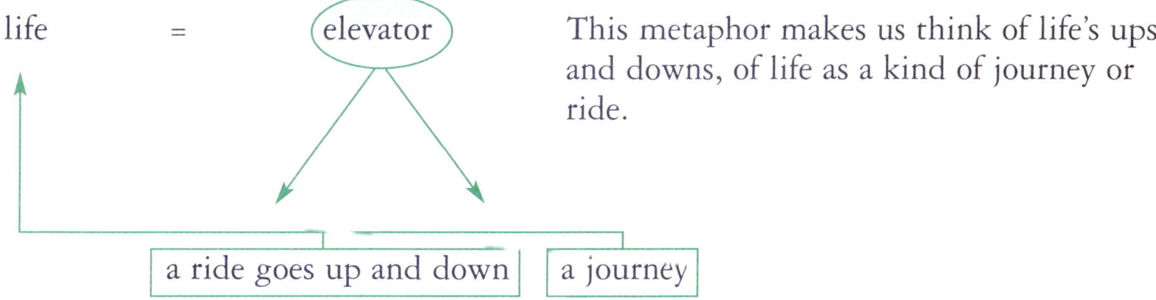

This metaphor makes us think of life's ups and downs, of life as a kind of journey or ride.

Answer the following questions in the space provided.

1. Arachne's fingers "flashed back and forth like lightning across the summer sky." What does this figure of speech suggest about Arachne's fingers and the way they moved?

2. The fabric that Arachne wove looked "like a field of wildflowers in the sunshine." What does this figure of speech suggest about the fabric that Arachne was weaving?

3. Athena's eyes blazed "like the sun on a hot day." What does this figure of speech suggest about Athena's eyes?

4. Myths are steppingstones into the world of the imagination. What does this figure of speech suggest about myths?

5. Facts are bridges into the world of scientific knowledge. What does this figure of speech suggest about facts?

6. Decide whether each figure of speech in items 1–5 above is a simile or a metaphor. Write the word *simile* or *metaphor* in the margin next to each item.

Scavenging for Words with the Old English Prefix *Be-*

The prefix *be-* has several uses and meanings. Sometimes *be-* adds these meanings to a root or base word: "to make or cause to become"; and "on, over, or around." You will find *be-* on verbs formed from nouns, adjectives, and other verbs. For example, the verb *belittle* is made from the adjective *little* and the prefix *be-*. Recognizing the word *little* in *belittle* will help you define *belittle*. The verb *befall* is made from the verb *fall* and *be-*. Recognizing the word *fall* in the word *befall* will help you define *befall*.

Search the myth for the highlighted word that best fits each definition. On the line, write that word. Each word begins with the prefix *be-*.

1. to look upon, especially to look upon something that is extraordinary: ____________
2. to say something that makes someone appear less important: ____________
3. to say something that stains or dirties someone's reputation: ____________
4. to happen to; to come to pass: ____________
5. to scold angrily and harshly: ____________
6. to give, as in giving a gift: ____________
7. dirty, shabby: ____________

Reviewing the Suffix *-Ful*

You have learned that the adjective suffix *-ful* means "full of." Something that is beautiful is full of beauty. Something that is colorful is full of color. Complete these sentences.

1. A fanciful tale is a tale that is ______________________________.
2. A person who is disrespectful is one who ______________________________.
3. A prideful person is one who ______________________________.
4. An all-powerful person is one who ______________________________.

Putting Words in Sentence Order 

Rewrite each sentence in the correct order. Use your understanding of the new vocabulary words as a clue. The words are grouped in phrases to help you, and the first phrase is in the correct order.

1. The young maiden
in ancient Greece | from the cities
lived in | a **remote** village
that was far

2. Arachne
that was magnificent | to **behold**
spun woolen threads | and wove **fabric**

3. When Arachne
that she owed her skill | to the goddess Athena,
heard someone say | she was **peeved**

4. The young weaver
thought that | to the **immortal** gods | she was superior

5. Arachne to the goddess Athena | to speak **disrespectfully** had a big **ego** | that caused her

6. When Athena and did not look | the **egocentric** young maiden, like a goddess | came to see she appeared **bedraggled**

7. Athena appeared of an old | and **bedraggled** woman | in the **guise**

8. The old woman warned, "Do not | **belittle** the gods. Do not | **besmirch** their reputations."

9. Athena **berated** that she was | only a **mortal** being the young maiden | and warned her

10. Athena would **befall** her | a terrible fate to **belittle** the gods | told the girl that if she continued

11. Arachne **resented** | spoke to her | that Athena | the words

12. Athena
the young maiden
her name on the city of Athens

to **berate**
because Athena was
an all-powerful goddess

had the right
who had **bestowed**

13. The all-powerful goddess
a colorful scene

with many figures
wove a magnificent **tapestry**

that included

14. The goddess
shrivel up

to make
smaller and smaller

had the power
and become

the young maiden

15. Today,
even though spiders

view spiders
with **repugnance,**

some people
are not always dangerous

G Writing Workshop—Writing Fanciful Myths

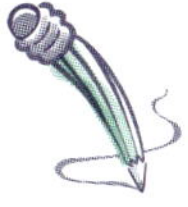

The ancient Greeks invented myths highlighting people's weaknesses and problems. The myths focused on gods and goddesses as they interacted with one another and with human beings. The Greeks had gods who were in charge of every aspect of their lives. Zeus was king of the gods; Hera, queen; Hades, god of the underworld and brother of Zeus; Poseidon, god of the sea and brother of Zeus; Aphrodite, goddess of love and beauty; Ares, god of war; Apollo, god of the sun and of poetry and song; and Hermes, messenger of the gods. Make up a fanciful tale in the style of a Greek myth. Remember that your myth should highlight a human weakness, such as greed or extremes of pride, envy, daring, or desire for revenge. Create a title that relates in some way to the weakness and use a dash in the title to highlight the weakness.

Reviewing What You Know
Lessons 7—11
Advanced Analytical Thinking and Investigative Skills

Solving Analogies

Select the answer that best completes each analogy. Write the answer on the line and fill in the correct circle. Take your time—these are tricky questions.

1. **spin : spinning wheel : : weave :** ______________

   Ⓐ fabric Ⓑ Arachne Ⓒ loom Ⓓ fine cloth

2. **pothole : hazard : : gate :** ______________

   Ⓐ barrier Ⓑ wood Ⓒ climb over Ⓓ tall

3. **accidentally : purposefully : : simultaneously :** ______________

   Ⓐ at the same time Ⓑ separately Ⓒ purposelessly Ⓓ on purpose

4. **renege : go back on : : recount :** ______________

   Ⓐ tell Ⓑ deceive Ⓒ disguise Ⓓ foretell the future

5. **bondage : a slave : : freedom :** ______________

   Ⓐ slavery Ⓑ impress Ⓒ a freedman Ⓓ liberty

6. **spectacular : plain : : considerable :** ______________

   Ⓐ many Ⓑ plane Ⓒ few Ⓓ exciting

7. **first name : George : : surname :** ______________

   Ⓐ personal name Ⓑ name Ⓒ Washington Ⓓ capital city

8. **myth : story : : German shepherd :** ______________

   Ⓐ dog Ⓑ tale Ⓒ tail Ⓓ fable

9. **vision : eyes : : hearing :** ______________

   Ⓐ vehicle Ⓑ feature Ⓒ ears Ⓓ sight

10. **weave : fabric : : spin :** ______________

Ⓐ loom Ⓑ spinning wheel Ⓒ thread Ⓓ fine cloth

11. **omnipresent : ubiquitous : : depressed :** ______________

Ⓐ everywhere Ⓑ many Ⓒ very sad Ⓓ unimpressed

12. **to corrode : to eat away : : to hitch :** ______________

Ⓐ to arch Ⓑ to connect Ⓒ to be foresighted Ⓓ to converse

13. **impressive : unimpressive : : near :** ______________

Ⓐ afar Ⓑ close by Ⓒ heavy Ⓓ extraordinary

14. **an enterprise : a business : : a feature :** ______________

Ⓐ a cause Ⓑ a reason Ⓒ a characteristic Ⓓ an explanation

15. **automobile : vehicle : : cellular telephone :** ______________

Ⓐ tower Ⓑ microphone Ⓒ spectator Ⓓ gadget

B Using the Dictionary to Distinguish Shades of Meaning

Look up these words in the dictionary: *permanent, lasting, unchanging, unwavering,* and *immortal*. It may help to look up the base words *last, changing, mortal,* and *wavering* as well as the longer words built from these bases. You may want to think about which words carry the most positive and the most negative connotations. Your teacher may let you work with a partner on this search-and-discover mission, because you will have to think long and hard about differences in word meanings.

1. What meaning do the words share?

2. What is the special meaning of the word *permanent* that distinguishes it from the other words in the set?

3. What is the special meaning of the word *lasting* that distinguishes it from the other words?

4. What is the special meaning of the word *unchanging* that distinguishes it from the other words?

5. What is the special meaning of the word *unwavering* that distinguishes it from the other words?

6. What is the special meaning of the word *immortal* that distinguishes it from the other words?

Assigning Feelings to Words—Positive and Negative Connotations

Next to each word or phrase, write either *positive connotation* or *negative connotation* depending on the kinds of feelings, or emotional messages, the words carry to you. Be ready to explain your choice.

1. deceive: ______________________________
2. hold in bondage: ______________________________
3. egocentric: ______________________________
4. immoral act: ______________________________
5. public nuisance: ______________________________
6. besmirch: ______________________________
7. renege: ______________________________
8. foresighted: ______________________________
9. ubiquitous: ______________________________
10. companionship: ______________________________

Write the following words from **most** positive to **least** positive in terms of the message they send to you. There is no right answer. This is a matter of personal opinion.

11. muscle man | giant of a man | strong man

12. iron-hearted | lion-hearted | strong | powerful

13. stuck | set in steel | fixed forever

14. curious | nosy | snoopy

15. nice | good | warmhearted

16. bad | terrible | repugnant

Dealing with Words that Have Multiple Meanings

The dictionary supplies numerous meanings for the word *cause*. Here are three:

- to make happen (a verb)
- the reason for an action or condition (a noun)
- a movement in which a person believes and for which he/she works hard (a noun)

Decide which meaning is correct in each of these sentences. Fill in the circle in front of the correct answer.

1. Marnie went to Washington to march for an important cause—equal payment for equal work regardless of gender or race.

   Ⓐ make happen   Ⓑ the reason for an action or condition

   Ⓒ a movement in which a person believes and for which he/she works hard

2. Marnie's actions cause me to wonder whether I should be more involved in national events.

Ⓐ make happen Ⓑ the reason for an action or condition

Ⓒ a movement in which a person believes and for which he/she works hard

3. The cause of her unhappiness was a cell phone ringing during her sister's wedding service.

Ⓐ make happen Ⓑ the reason for an action or condition

Ⓒ a movement in which a person believes and for which he/she works hard

Paraphrasing by Expressing Ideas in Different Words

Rewrite the following sentences using different words.

1. The soldiers endured hardships as they wintered in the barren encampment.

2. The student reached a turning point in her life.

3. The weaver lived in a remote village.

4. Athena berated the egocentric maiden.

5. The veteran applied for a pension.

6. My cat loves to play pranks.

7. The general wore a granite face as he barked out his orders.

8. When she heard that she had passed the test, Helga was as carefree as a bluebird on a bright summer morning.

Reread items 7 and 8.

9. Which is an example of a metaphor?

10. Which is an example of a simile?

F Reviewing the Meaning and Use of Roots and Affixes

Above each arrow, write the meaning of the word element and another word that is built with that element.

1. tele ↑ vision ↑

2. spect ↑ ac ular ↑

3. phono ↑ graph ↑

4. fore ↑ sighted ↑

5. credit ↑

6. con ↑ verse ↑

G Reviewing Interesting Words

Write the letter of the definition on the line in front of the correct word.

Group One: Verbs

____ 1. to yearn	a. to dislike intensely
____ 2. to abhor	b. to tell
____ 3. to envision	c. to see
____ 4. to recount	d. to soil, especially to dirty someone's reputation
____ 5. to behold	e. to picture in the mind
____ 6. to besmirch	f. to crave; to long for something
____ 7. to shrivel up	g. to get smaller and smaller and dry up

Group Two: Nouns

____ 8. a tapestry	h. the self
____ 9. the ego	i. a cloth woven with designs and pictures
____ 10. a phenomenon	j. someone or something that takes the place of another
____ 11. a substitute	k. servitude
____ 12. bondage	l. a means
____ 13. a vehicle	m. the ability to move
____ 14. mobility	n. an unusual, extraordinary event or occurrence
____ 15. vision	o. sight

Group Three: Adjectives

___ 16. foremost	p. related to sight and seeing
___ 17. accidental	q. first in rank or status; outstanding
___ 18. visual	r. by chance; not on purpose
___ 19. dependent	s. against everything right and good
___ 20. immoral	t. not able to stand on your own feet; not able to manage by yourself
___ 21. ubiquitous	u. happening at the same time
___ 22. simultaneous	v. lasting forever; never dying
___ 23. rotary	w. turning round and round
___ 24. immortal	x. found everywhere to the point of becoming a nuisance

Writing Workshop—Considering What Is Important

In Part 2 of this book, you learned about these topics:

- Morris Frank, a person with vision who saw the potential of seeing-eye dogs
- the intelligence of dolphins
- African Americans who served the cause of freedom during the Revolutionary War
- wireless telecommunication, an example of human inventiveness
- the Greek myth of Arachne, an example of how ancient people tried to explain their world before the development of science and technology

From reading these accounts, what have you learned about what is important in living a good life? Discuss with several other students what you have learned. Then write your ideas during Writing Workshop.

Part 3

The Roots Uni-, Bi-, Tri-/Ter-, Quart-, Quadr-, Deca-, Cent-, and Anni-/Enni-

Making Latin and Italian Word Connections

Read the following story to find out more about the way words are put together and about the origins of English words.

Check the Numbers

Have you ever heard people describing the **bicentennial** of the United States? The American bicentennial took place on July 4, 1976. On this day the country celebrated the 200th **anniversary** of the nation's birth. There were fireworks in parks across the country, parades in cities and towns, and speeches about the importance of freedom. People **rejoiced** as they thought about the events of July 4, 1776. They were glad that the United States had **survived** for two hundred years as a free, democratic country. Few democratic countries have existed, or have continued to be, independent nations for that long. Can you calculate when the United States will celebrate its **tercentennial**, or tricentennial? That is an easy task if you apply your knowledge of word elements and make a simple arithmetic calculation. Start by considering the **components** of the word *bicentennial* as shown here:

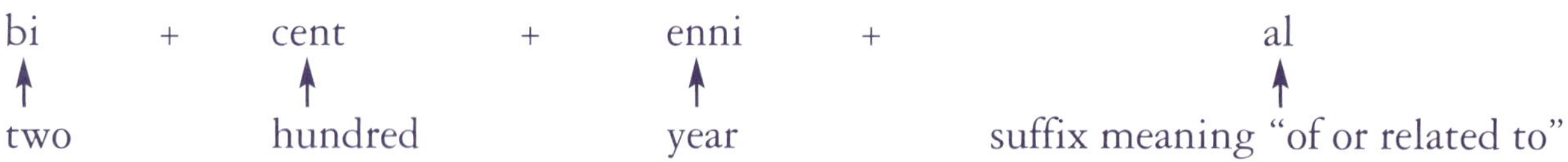

You can see the meaning of *bicentennial* "right there" within the word itself:

- *Bi-* contributes the meaning "two."
- *Cent-* adds the meaning "hundred."
- *Enni-* (often appearing as *anni-*, as in *anniversary*) contributes the idea of "year."
- The suffix *-al* allows you to say that *bicentennial* relates to a two-hundred-year anniversary. You see this suffix also on the word ***annual***, meaning "yearly or related to a period of a year."

Let's lay out the word *tercentennial* (or *tricentennial*) in the same way:

ter (or tri)	+	cent	+	enni	+	al
↑		↑		↑		↑
three		hundred		year		suffix meaning "of or related to"

All you have to do is add 300 to 1776 to figure out that the United States will celebrate its tercentennial on July 4, 2076. You may be alive in 2076 to enjoy the celebration. To do that, you will have to hang around for more than six **decades**. Now recall the meaning of *decade* by remembering that *dec-* or *deci-* means "ten." By making this connection, you can figure out that a decade is a period of ten years.

The **pursuit** of word connections and derivations can be exciting. For example, let's follow the trail found within another big word—***quarantine***. *Quarantine* is derived from an Italian word for "forty." Today we use *quarantine* to mean "a period of time when people must be **isolated**, or kept apart, from others because they have a contagious disease." That meaning comes from the fact that during the Middle Ages, ships entering a harbor were **prohibited** from immediately unloading their **cargo** and the people on board. Instead, the ships had to sit in the harbor for 40 days—in quarantine—before the goods could be unloaded and the people could get off.

You may recall some common words, such as *quart* and *quarter*, that are related to the word *quarantine*. These words contain either the root *quart-* or *quadr-*, both of which mean "four." You can tell just by looking at *quart-* and *quadr-* that both roots are connected to the Italian word for forty (*quaranta*). Other words begin with these roots. For example, you may have been a member of a ***quartet***, a singing or instrumental group with four people. There is also the word ***quadrangle***, a four-sided courtyard usually surrounded by buildings. You may walk across a quadrangle when you visit a **university**. A university is a big school that people attend after leaving high school. By the way, do you see the element *uni-* in the word *university*? You may recall that *uni-* means "one." You also see *uni-* on words such as *unique, unite,* and *union*.

If you enjoy investigating words such as *university, bicentennial, tercentennial, quadrangle, quarantine,* and *decade*, you might want to become a **linguist** after you graduate from a university. Linguists study languages; they investigate where words come from and how words are interrelated. In short, they are word detectives.

Thinking about Ideas and Relationships

Next to each root, write its meaning. If you have trouble remembering, refer to the article you just read and/or your dictionary.

1. uni-:
2. bi-:
3. tri-/ter-:
4. quart-:
5. quadr-:
6. deci-:
7. cent-:
8. anni- (or enni-):

B Becoming a Word Detective

Fill in the circle in front of the best answer. You have not studied all the words, but you can figure out the answers based on what you know about word elements.

1. If the word *annual* means "yearly," what does ***biannual*** mean?

   Ⓐ happening twice a year Ⓑ happening every year
   Ⓒ happening once in a while Ⓓ never happening

2. If the root *linqua* means "language or tongue," what does ***bilingual*** mean?

   Ⓐ unable to speak a language Ⓑ able to speak a language
   Ⓒ able to speak two languages Ⓓ able to speak three languages

3. If *polygon* refers to a shape that has many sides, what is a ***decagon***?

   Ⓐ a circle Ⓑ a triangle Ⓒ a square Ⓓ a ten-sided shape

4. If you triple something, you multiply it by three. What do you do when you **quadruple** something?

   Ⓐ multiple it by four   Ⓑ divide it by four

   Ⓒ multiply it by ten   Ⓓ divide it by ten

5. If a mother gives birth to quadruplets, she has four children at one time. How many children does she have if she has **triplets**?

   Ⓐ two   Ⓑ three   Ⓒ four   Ⓓ five

6. How many **centimeters** are there in a meter?

   Ⓐ one   Ⓑ two   Ⓒ ten   Ⓓ one hundred

7. A **decimal** system is based on what number?

   Ⓐ one   Ⓑ ten   Ⓒ one hundred   Ⓓ one thousand

8. How many years are there in a **century**?

   Ⓐ one   Ⓑ two   Ⓒ ten   Ⓓ one hundred

9. How many horns are there on the mythical animal called a **unicorn**?

   Ⓐ none   Ⓑ one   Ⓒ two   Ⓓ three

10. How many **quarts** are in a gallon?

    Ⓐ two   Ⓑ four   Ⓒ ten   Ⓓ twelve

11. How are the words ***bicentennial*** and ***millennium*** connected?

    Ⓐ both start with the same prefix

    Ⓑ both are based on the same root (*anni-/enni-*), meaning "year"

    Ⓒ both end with the same suffix

    Ⓓ both have the same number of syllables

12. How are the words ***anniversary*** and ***annual*** connected? Before you answer, think about the meanings of the words *prefix* and *root*.

    Ⓐ both start with the same prefix

    Ⓑ both are based on the same root (*anni-/enni-*), meaning "year"

    Ⓒ both end with the same suffix

    Ⓓ both have the same number of syllables

C Defining Related Words

Write the letter of the definition on the line in front of each word.

Group One: Adjectives and Nouns

___ 1. bicentennial	a. happening yearly
___ 2. tercentennial	b. happening twice in a year
___ 3. annual	c. a three-hundred-year anniversary
___ 4. biannual	d. a one-hundred-year anniversary
___ 5. centennial	e. a two-hundred-year anniversary
___ 6. decade	f. a period of ten years

Group Two: Nouns and Verbs

___ 7. rejoice	g. the act of going after someone or something
___ 8. pursuit	h. to not allow; forbid
___ 9. quarantine	i. to take great joy in
___ 10. prohibit	j. a period when a person is not allowed to be with other people to prevent disease from spreading
___ 11. survive	k. to keep apart from others
___ 12. isolate	l. to continue to exist, to last despite problems

Group Three: Nouns

___ 13. university	m. a four-sided, open area surrounded by buildings
___ 14. linguist	n. the yearly return of a special date, such as a birthday or wedding
___ 15. quadrangle	o. a choral or instrumental group made up of four people
___ 16. quartet	p. a part of something else; an element contained within something else
___ 17. cargo	q. a person who studies languages; a word detective
___ 18. component	r. goods carried on a ship or airplane
___ 19. anniversary	s. a school for advanced study after high school

STRATEGY CENTER

When you encounter unfamiliar multisyllabic words, look for shorter words or component parts within them that you already know. Use your knowledge of the shorter words or components to help you hypothesize the meaning of the unfamiliar word.

Writing Sentences

1. In your notebook, write sentences with each of these nouns: *cargo, linguist, pursuit, quarantine, university, quartet, quadrangle, bicentennial, decade,* and *component*. You can use the plural forms of the nouns if you prefer. (Hint: Use *quarantine* within the prepositional phrase *in quarantine*.)

2. With a partner, make up sentences with the verbs *isolate, survive, rejoice,* and *prohibit*. You can write your sentences in the past tense if you prefer. Record them in your notebook.

Writing Workshop

Become a linguist, a word detective. Make a linguistic study of a pair of related words. Write a paragraph in which you explain the connection between the words. For example, you could explain the connection between the words *university* and *universal, biannual* and *biennial*, *anniversary* and *annual*, *anniversary* and *universal*, *linguist* and *linguistics*, *pursue* and *pursuit*, or *rejoice* and *joy*. Check several dictionaries to research your topic.

Idioms
Looking at Odd, or Strange, Uses of Ordinary Words

As you enjoy the following story, think about the idioms that give the story a bit of "color." Of course, you know that good writers do not overuse idioms. In this case, the author has used lots of idioms so that you learn some fun examples of idiomatic speech.

Talking Turkey—Telling It Like It Is

My Grandfather Artie is always giving me advice—pointers on how to get ahead. One day he sat me down to **talk turkey**—to tell me just exactly what I had to do to be a success. When Grandpa Artie began, he did not **beat around the bush**. He came right to the point and said, "I advise you to **take a leaf out of my book**, to follow my example. First, I have found that it is important to **strike while the iron is hot**. If you do not take advantage of a good opportunity when it comes along, you may be **left out in the cold**. You will be shut out and left in a position where you do not know what is going on.

"You often must **take the bull by the horns**. You must jump right in and take action. Don't hold back. Also, when you lose a race or when you have failed, **take it on the chin**. Don't be defeated by your loss. Don't **take a powder**. It never pays to run away from failure or defeat."

Grandpa Artie stopped for a moment, and then he continued, "I don't want to **take the wind out of your sails**. I don't mean to make you feel badly or stop you dead in your tracks, but I am not **talking through my hat**. I know what I am talking about because I have **been there and done that**. I have had a lot of experiences in life—good and bad. I have seen what can happen in this world. I intend to **take you under my wing** and look after you when life gets rough.

"Well," Grandpa Artie said, "Here are some more words of wisdom.

"Be careful not to **blow a fuse** when someone tells you that you are wrong. It doesn't pay to get really mad and tell that person off. You may be **at the end of your rope**—you may be ready to burst and think that you cannot take any more criticism. But think before you speak or strike out at someone. Hold your tongue, even though you feel that you are caught **between a rock and a hard place**—that you are trapped in a tight spot and have nowhere to turn. I'm not telling you to take everything lying down. No way. At some point, you must stand up and be counted. Still, when you do speak out, do it in a polite way. Think about what you are saying and how the other person must feel."

I sat back and looked at my grandfather. I knew I was hearing this advice **straight from the horse's mouth**. It was the truth, not sugar-coated at all, because Grandpa Artie knows what he is talking about. He always gets it right. When I looked at my grandfather, he looked me straight in the eyes and said, "**That's the way the ball bounces**. That's the way life is! Bounce with it and you will succeed."

A Thinking about Ideas and Relationships

1. What kind of a person is Grandpa Artie? Give some examples from the story to support your answer, and use some idioms in your explanation.

2. Given the way the ball bounces, which piece of Grandpa Artie's advice do you think is most important to get ahead in today's world? Explain your choice.

3. Would you want to have a relative who is like Grandpa Artie? Give some reasons to support your opinion.

Clarifying the Meanings of Idioms through Drawing

For each idiom, draw a picture showing its literal interpretation. Next to your picture, write the actual interpretation. By *literal interpretation*, we mean what is communicated if you take the words at face value, word for word. By *actual interpretation*, we mean what the person is trying to say—his or her intended meaning.

1. take the bull by the horns

2. get advice straight from the horse's mouth

3. take a powder

4. caught between a rock and a hard place

5. beat around the bush

6. blow a fuse

7. take someone under your wing

Getting the Actual Meaning of Idioms

Complete the following table by writing down the actual meanings of the idioms—what the person is actually saying.

Idioms	Actual Meanings of the Idioms
1. talk turkey	
2. take a leaf out of someone's book	
3. strike while the iron is hot	
4. find yourself left out in the cold	
5. take it on the chin	
6. take the wind out of your sails	
7. talk through your hat	
8. been there and done that	
9. be at the end of your rope	
10. that's the way the ball bounces	

Matching Idioms with Their Actual Meanings

Write the letter of the definition on the line in front of each idiom.

Group One: Idioms

___ 1. talk turkey	a. take action right away
___ 2. beat around the bush	b. left out of the action
___ 3. take a leaf from someone's book	c. run away
___ 4. take a powder	d. follow someone's example
___ 5. find yourself left out in the cold	e. not come directly to the point
___ 6. take the bull by the horns	f. tell it as it is; come directly to the point

Group Two: More Idioms

___ 7. take it on the chin	g. grasp the opportunity to take action
___ 8. strike while the iron's hot	h. take a punishment without crying
___ 9. take the wind out of your sails	i. say something without really knowing what you are talking about
___ 10. talk through your hat	j. make you feel badly; make you feel defeated
___ 11. been there and done that	k. take care of or look after someone
___ 12. take someone under your wing	l. have had that experience before

Group Three: And More Idioms

___ 13. blow your fuse	m. have had about all you can take
___ 14. be at the end of your rope	n. learn from someone who knows
___ 15. caught between a rock and a hard place	o. the way life is
___ 16. hear it straight from the horse's mouth	p. get really angry and explode
___ 17. that's the way the ball bounces	q. be in a tight spot

E Writing Workshop

Did anyone ever talk turkey to you and give you some good advice? Write about it. Or write about a time when you were caught between a rock and a hard place, when someone took the wind out of your sails, when you were at the end of your rope, or when you thought it wise to take a powder. Use a few idioms to add "color" to your writing.

Prefixes That Say "No Way" or "All Wrong"

Making More Word Connections

Listen to this report to find out why it is important for everyone to be able to read and write.

Too Many Poor Readers and Writers in the United States!

News Update! In 2002, an important research study reported on **illiteracy** among adults in the United States. According to this recent study,[1] 92 million adult Americans have difficulty reading and writing. Some of these adults have a **disability**, a condition that keeps them from learning to read or write as most people can. Many, however, have never had the opportunity to learn to read and write well. Some function, or perform, at a very low reading level, and are **unable** to fill out a job application or to understand what they read.

While this may sound **incredible** in a country like the United States, unfortunately, the results of the study are **irrefutable**. No one can argue that the study's findings are false. The findings are based on research done over a number of years.

Obviously, those people who are **illiterate** face **immense** problems. They may have trouble getting and keeping good jobs. Most jobs that pay decent wages require strong reading and writing skills. As a result, people without these important skills suffer **disproportionately** compared with the rest of the population. In other words, their chances of getting and keeping good jobs are much lower than the rest of the population's. However, illiteracy also affects the entire population, at least **indirectly**. How?

We live in a democracy, in which the power resides with the voters. Citizens who are **nonfunctional** as readers lack the ability to keep up with important issues and vote on them. By nonfunctional, we mean not having the ability to function or perform in today's technologically advanced society.

Don't **misinterpret** what you just read. An illiterate person is not always **nonproductive**. Being illiterate does not mean that a person cannot add to society or have input into it.

1. The study was conducted by the National Adult Literacy Survey, 2002.

Being illiterate does not mean that a person is **irresponsible** and never takes responsibility for his or her actions. It would be a **misconception**—a mistaken idea—to think that. People should never face the **indignity** of being put in a situation where they feel worthless because of their inability to read and write. It *is* hard to have one's pride taken away.

Illiteracy remains a major problem in our country, one that we must all take to heart. We should have no **misgivings** about trying to reduce illiteracy among adults. Without a doubt, our society cannot remain **indifferent**. We cannot stand by, bury our heads in the sand, and do nothing about such an **unacceptable** situation.

As individuals, we should not **misdirect** our energy toward **unessential** things and spend too much time on unimportant activities. Each one of us must make the effort to develop strong reading and writing skills. We must spend our time wisely, reading worthwhile books, newspapers, and magazines. By doing this, we invest in the future. We are using our time today in a way that will help everyone tomorrow.

Thinking about Ideas and Relationships

1. What is the major finding of the research study of the National Adult Literacy Survey?

2. Why is it hard on people to be illiterate in today's world?

3. What conclusion can you draw from the report that you can apply to your life?

Making Connections among Words

1. Study the bold-faced words in the news report. Decide: How are these words similar in meaning? Write your hypothesis here and be ready to explain your findings—what you have discovered.

2. Working with a partner, make a web with these words from the article grouped into branches that show the relationships among the words: *illiteracy, illiterate, disability, unable, nonfunctional, disproportionately, unessential, irrefutable, irresponsible, indignity, indirectly, misdirect, nonproductive, misgivings, immense, incredible, unacceptable, misinterpret, misconception,* and *indifferent*. At the center of the web, write down the feature shared by the words. In your notebook, write a definition of each word. You can build your definitions around the base word and the prefix you see in the word. For example, you can define *unable* as "not able." If you hit a snag, check a dictionary or context clues in the report.

Using Context Clues and Word Elements to Understand Big Words

Write the letter of the definition on the line in front of each word.

Group One (Remember that the prefixes *un-*, *dis-*, and *non* mean "not.")

___ 1. unable	a. not important
___ 2. unacceptable	b. not productive
___ 3. unessential	c. not able to operate or function
___ 4. nonproductive	d. not acceptable
___ 5. nonfunctional	e. a condition in which one is not able to function or perform well
___ 6. disability	f. not able
___ 7. disproportionate	g. not related to what the facts should be; out of proportion

Group Two (Remember that one meaning of the prefix *in-/im-/il-/ir-* is "not.")

___ 8. irrefutable	h. not able to be denied
___ 9. irresponsible	i. large
___ 10. indifferent	j. not directly
___ 11. indirectly	k. not able to be believed; unbelievable
___ 12. incredible	l. not able to read or write
___ 13. indignity	m. the condition of not being able to read or write
___ 14. immense	n. not taking responsibility
___ 15. illiterate	o. not caring
___ 16. illiteracy	p. an action or way of being treated that makes a person feel worthless

Group Three (Remember that the prefix *mis-* means "bad, wrong, badly, wrongly.")

___ 17. misgivings	q. to send or go in the wrong direction
___ 18. misinterpret	r. feelings of doubt or distrust
___ 19. misdirect	s. to figure out incorrectly
___ 20. misconceptions	t. mistaken thoughts or ideas

Using Your Knowledge of New Words to Understand What People Are Saying

Complete the sentences.

1. If I have **misgivings** about something that I did, I ______________________________.
2. If you **misinterpret** what I say, you ______________________________.
3. If you find what I do **unacceptable**, then you ______________________________.
4. If I tell you that I spent a **nonproductive** afternoon, then you know that ______________________________.
5. If I am **indifferent** to the **indignities** that some people suffer because they are **illiterate**, I am ______________________________.
6. If I give you **irrefutable** proof that I am innocent, you ______________________________.
7. If I spend a **disproportionately** large amount of time doing **unessential** things, I ______________________________.
8. If I **misdirect** my efforts and fail to complete an easy task you have assigned to me, I ______________________________.
9. If I become **nonfunctional** in an emergency, I ______________________________.
10. If I tell you that something **incredible** happened to me, you ______________________________.
11. If I have a writing **disability**, I ______________________________.
12. If I develop an **immense misconception** after reading a news report, I ______________________________.
13. If I explain that **illiteracy** is very high in a country, you know that ______________________________.
14. If I function **irresponsibly** in carrying out a task you assign, I ______________________________.

Writing Workshop

Do you have any ideas about what you might want to do when you leave school? Do you know what you must do to achieve your goal? Spend a little time reading about a career you might want to pursue in the future and what kind of training is required. Then write a short report explaining about that career and why you have chosen it.

16 The Prefixes Trans-, Pre-, and Post- and the Root Mit-/Mis-

Investigating More Word Connections

Listen to find out how two scientists **transformed** people's conception of how one deadly disease is **transmitted**. Discover how Carlos Juan Finlay and Jesse William Lazear changed people's ideas of how yellow fever is passed from one person to the next.

Two Scientists Who Changed How We Think about Yellow Fever

Have you ever gone out to play on a warm summer evening and found a mosquito on your arm? You probably slapped it away, but too late! The mosquito had already bitten you and sucked up some of your blood.

If you live in most parts of North America, you would not be too upset about a mosquito bite. You would probably wash the itchy spot and perhaps rub on an antibiotic to prevent an infection or some cream to stop the itching. Soon the redness would disappear. Having experienced a mosquito bite, the next time you went outside to play, you might decide to use a mosquito **repellent**—a substance that is irritating to insects and turns them away.

You would have had more reasons to be upset if you had been bitten in Cuba during the 1800s and early 1900s. At that time, yellow fever was **prevalent** in Cuba. The disease was everywhere. During an **epidemic** when many people **contracted**, or caught, yellow fever, you might have become very sick with the disease as a result of just one mosquito bite.

Today, we know that one kind of mosquito is responsible for the **transmission** of yellow fever. This mosquito carries the tiny organisms that cause the disease; it **transfers** them, or moves them, from one person to another. When a female mosquito bites someone who has yellow fever, it sucks up the disease-causing organisms. If after about twelve days that same mosquito bites another human being, it passes the dangerous organisms to that person. As a result, that person contracts yellow fever.

In the past, many people had the misconception that yellow fever was transmitted through dirty bedclothes or on air currents. Carlos Juan Finlay, a great Cuban doctor, suggested the **premise** that mosquitoes were the carriers of yellow fever. Unfortunately, many people rejected Dr. Finlay's basic idea. They had a **preconception**; they already had an idea in their heads, and they found it hard to believe anything else.

Carlos Juan Finlay set out to prove his premise—his hypothesis—by running tests on human volunteers. Dr. Finlay could do this because he lived at a time that **predated** today's rules about experimenting on human beings. Between 1881 and 1900, the doctor raised female mosquitoes and had them bite people who had yellow fever. He then had the same mosquitoes bite 102 volunteers. Some of those volunteers developed a mild case of the disease. This seemed to suggest a connection between mosquitoes and yellow fever. However, people continued to ask, "Why don't all the volunteers bitten by infected mosquitoes contract the disease?"

Dr. Jesse William Lazear found the answer. Lazear went to Cuba in 1900 as part of an American Commission to study yellow fever. First, he carefully reread Finlay's laboratory notebooks. After doing that, he raised his own mosquitoes and infected those insects for use in his laboratory—his scientific workshop. Then Lazear infected human volunteers over a period of twenty days after the mosquitoes were infected. He found that only volunteers bitten toward the end of the twenty-day period got yellow fever.

Lazear had made a major discovery. He had found out that there is a lag time, or a delay, between when a mosquito sucks up disease-carrying organisms from a sick person and when that mosquito can infect another person. As Lazear learned, it takes twelve or more days for the yellow fever organism to grow and develop in a mosquito. Only after twelve days have passed can a bite from an infected mosquito infect another person with yellow fever.

A short time later, Lazear contracted yellow fever and died. He was 34 years old. Walter Reed was the head of the American Commission in Cuba. Dr. Reed read Lazear's first notebook, "Yellow Fever—A **Preliminary** Note." Reed found evidence that Lazear may have used himself as a guinea pig.[1] Although we are not sure, Lazear may have let an infected mosquito bite his own arm to prove that mosquitoes transmit yellow fever.

Carlos Finlay and Jesse Lazear transformed scientists' ideas about yellow fever. What happened back then—what **transpired** in these doctors' laboratories—changed how scientists view yellow fever. It also helped scientists figure out how to prevent the disease. For these reasons, we can truly say that Carlos Finlay and Jesse Lazear made major contributions to **posterity**—to future generations who came after them.

And now for a **postscript**—an afterthought: Today, you can be inoculated against yellow fever. Some countries—such as Brazil where cases of yellow fever still appear—require you to be inoculated if you want to visit there.

1. The phrase "to use yourself as a guinea pig" is an idiom. It means "to use yourself as a volunteer in an experiment you are running."

Thinking about Ideas and Relationships

1. How is yellow fever transmitted?

2. Why did other people find it hard to believe Carlos Juan Finlay's premise about the transmission of yellow fever?

Researching Word Connections and Derivations

Work with one or two partners to complete these projects.

1. Today, with the outbreak of mosquito-carried diseases (such as the West Nile Virus), many people use insect repellent when they go outside in the summer. What root do you see in the word *repellent*? What is a repellent? What other words are related to the word *repellent*? Check a dictionary for answers and write your responses in your notebook.

2. The word *contract* has multiple meanings and can be used as both a noun and a verb. Check the meanings, uses, and derivation of *contract* in an advanced dictionary. Then make a chart in your notebook in which you outline the word's meanings, uses, and derivation. Also see if you can identify other words that are related to *contract*.

3. There have been many epidemics throughout the world. Use an advanced dictionary to investigate the meaning of the word *epidemic* and its Greek derivation. You may have to check several dictionaries to locate one that gives the complete derivation.

Webbing Related Words

Complete the following projects in your notebook or on a large sheet of chart paper.

1. Create a web of words that begin with the prefix *pre-*. Write *pre-* and its meanings in the center of the web. Record words with the prefix at the ends of spokes extending from the center. On the web, include a definition and a sample sentence with each word you record. Start with words from this lesson. Use a dictionary to locate others.
2. Create a similar word web using the prefix *post-*.
3. Create a word web using the prefix *trans-*.

STRATEGY CENTER

When you meet an unfamiliar word:

- Check the context for clues to meaning.
- Check components of the word to see if they supply useful clues (such as *pre-*, *trans-*, and *post-*).
- Check the dictionary for definitions in cases where you are still uncertain.
- Decide which one of the dictionary definitions fits the context in which the word is used. Don't overlook the derivation section of a dictionary entry. It supplies interesting information.

Reviewing the Lesson Words

Find the BEST word or group of words to define the highlighted word, complete each sentence, or answer the question. Then fill in the circle in front of your answer.

1. Yellow fever is **transmitted** by mosquitoes.

   Ⓐ carried from one person or place to another Ⓑ created

   Ⓒ worked upon Ⓓ misconceived

2. Many people use **repellent** when they go outside during the summer.

   Ⓐ sunscreen Ⓑ an antibiotic

   Ⓒ something that repels insects Ⓓ caution

3. If you **transform** something, you ________________.

   Ⓐ repeat it Ⓑ change it Ⓒ work on it Ⓓ deliver it

4. If something is **prevalent**, it is ________________.

   Ⓐ important Ⓑ not important Ⓒ very common Ⓓ nowhere

5. What happens during an **epidemic**?

   Ⓐ many people get rich quickly

   Ⓑ many people contract the same deadly disease

   Ⓒ many people have episodes of coughing

   Ⓓ many people go to school

6. For many years, scientists did not know what was responsible for the **transmission** of yellow fever.

   Ⓐ spread of the disease from one person to another Ⓑ creation

   Ⓒ preconception Ⓓ misconception

7. When you **transfer** something, you ________________.

   Ⓐ eat it Ⓑ enjoy it

   Ⓒ move it from one person or place to another Ⓓ manufacture it

8. Dr. Finlay's **premise** was that the mosquito was responsible for the transmission of yellow fever.

Ⓐ procedure Ⓑ basic idea Ⓒ question Ⓓ criticism

9. Sometimes a person's **preconception** blocks progress.

Ⓐ idea already held Ⓑ misbehavior
Ⓒ selfishness Ⓓ kindness

10. His year of birth **predates** mine. This means that ________________.

Ⓐ he is older than I am. Ⓑ he is younger than I am. Ⓒ we are the same age.

11. The scientist made **preliminary** notes. She made those notes ________________.

Ⓐ before really starting her experiment Ⓑ in the middle of her experiment
Ⓒ just before ending her experiment Ⓓ after the experiment was all over

12. I never found out what **transpired** that day.

Ⓐ happened Ⓑ transferred Ⓒ transformed Ⓓ transmitted

13. Miranda added a **postscript** to her letter.

Ⓐ a note at the beginning Ⓑ a note in the middle Ⓒ a note at the end

14. Dr. Finlay made a contribution to **posterity**.

Ⓐ people who come before Ⓑ people who live at the same time
Ⓒ people who come after Ⓓ people who have died

15. When you **contract** a deadly disease, you ________________.

Ⓐ get better from it Ⓑ suffer from it
Ⓒ catch, or get it Ⓓ pass it on to someone else

E Writing Workshop

Carlos Juan Finlay and Jesse William Lazear are "unsung heroes." We do not often hear of them, and yet these men have made great contributions to posterity. Do you know of an unsung hero—someone who did something worthwhile but who may not have been recognized for his or her contribution? It could be a family member or a friend. Write about that unsung hero during workshop.

The Prefixes Inter-, Trans-, and Circum-

Picturing Ideas

Read to discover how the locks in the Panama Canal work. Keep visualizing what is happening as a ship passes through the locks of a canal. Also find out why the Panama Canal is still such an important interocean connection.

The First Trip through the Panama Canal

August 15, 1914. On that day a small passenger and cargo ship named the SS *Ancon* pulled into the first **lock** on the Atlantic/Caribbean side of the Panama Canal. There was not much water in the lock. Then the giant doors of the lock swung closed behind the SS *Ancon*, and millions of gallons of water began to pour into the rectangular, box-like lock. As the water poured in, the SS *Ancon* slowly began to rise until the ship was many feet higher than when it had first entered the lock.

When the water stopped coming in, the giant doors in front of the SS *Ancon* swung open, and the ship entered the second lock. There, the process was repeated. The doors closed behind the ship, water poured into the lock, the SS *Ancon* floated upward with the rising water, the front doors of the lock swung open, and the ship moved out of the second lock and into the next one in the series. Here the same thing happened for a third time. As the SS *Ancon* went through the three locks, the ship was raised 85 feet (or 26 m.).

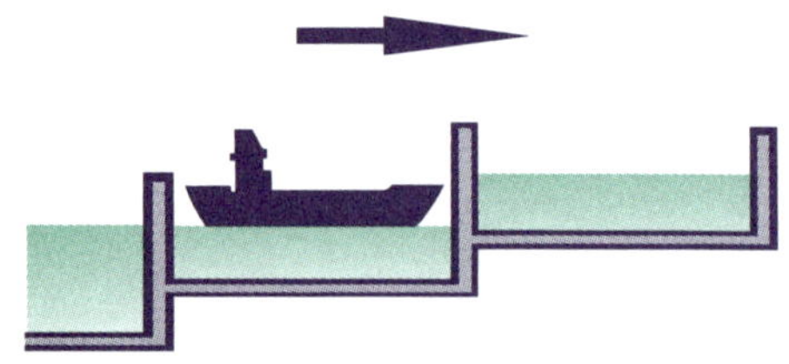

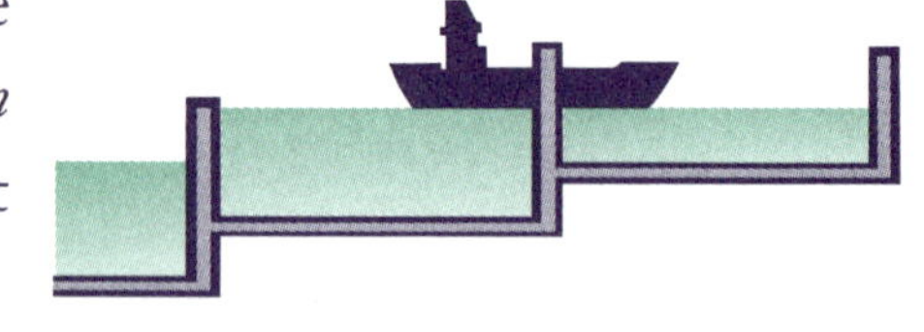

The SS *Ancon* then steamed across Gatun Lake. Gatun is a large, man-made lake. The engineers formed it by building a dam across the powerful Chagres River.

The ship steamed on through the Gaillard Cut. As the captain of the SS *Ancon* navigated the ship through the cut, he saw low-lying mountains on either side. In this part of the canal, the builders had dug a **trench**, or channel, through the **Continental Divide**. The Continental Divide is a series of **intercontinental** mountain ranges. These ranges begin in northern Canada in North America and go all the way to the tip of South America. Engineers had blasted away solid rock to build the trench that **intersects**, or cuts across, the Continental Divide, which extends like a spine down the center of Panama.

Once through the Gaillard Cut, the ship entered another group of locks on the Pacific Ocean side of the canal. Here, what happened on the Atlantic side of the canal was reversed. The SS *Ancon* entered the first lock, which this time was filled to the top with water. The doors of the lock swung closed behind the ship, the water in the lock was drained out, and the vessel was lowered 31 feet (or 9 m.). Then the doors of the lock in front of the ship swung open, and the SS *Ancon* moved into a short channel leading to two more locks. Again the SS *Ancon* entered a lock filled with water, the doors behind the ship were closed, the water level was lowered, and the ship floated downward. The same thing happened as the SS *Ancon* entered the last lock. Finally, the doors swung open on the last lock, and the SS *Ancon* steamed out of the canal into the Pacific Ocean. The SS *Ancon* had **transited** the Panama Canal in a little under nine hours. It was the first ship ever to have done this.

The transit of the SS *Ancon* through the Panama Canal marked the fulfillment of a dream. That dream was to build an interocean canal across the Isthmus of Panama to connect the Atlantic Ocean to the Pacific Ocean. An **isthmus** is a narrow strip of land that links two larger landmasses. The need for such an **interconnecting** canal was great. Until that day in 1914, ships had to **circumnavigate**—circle all around—South America to go from New York to San Francisco. Under these **circumstances**, the trip was very long. Nothing could be done to **circumvent** a lengthy ocean voyage if a ship wanted to travel from New York to San Francisco.

In the early 1900s, the French had tried to build a canal through the Isthmus of Panama by digging a big sea-level ditch, or trench. The French failed because diseases such as yellow fever and malaria were prevalent. During their attempt to build a canal, 22,000 workers died, most of them from deadly diseases. The French also failed because there was just too much rock and dirt to **excavate**. There was too much material to dig and carry away in order to cut the mountains of the Continental Divide down to sea level.

When the Americans arrived in 1904 to take over where the French had left off, they made two decisions. First, they decided to **eradicate** the mosquitoes that transmitted yellow fever and malaria. To get rid of these insects, the Americans went into the interior of the country to drain the swamps where mosquitoes lived. They cut down jungles and they sprayed **insecticides**—chemicals that killed the mosquitoes.

Second, the Americans decided to build a canal with locks. In this kind of canal, locks raise a ship on one side of a landmass and lower it on the other side. By doing this in Panama, the American engineers avoided the problem of blasting and excavating the rock and dirt all the way down to sea level.

These decisions proved to be smart ones. Today, the Panama Canal is an important **international** shipping link— a major transportation **interconnection** that brings nations closer together. It stands as a monument to people's determination to try to conquer the unconquerable.

Thinking about Ideas and Interrelationships

1. Why is the Panama Canal such an important transportation link or interconnection?

2. Why did the French fail in their attempt to build a canal across the Isthmus of Panama?

3. Why did the Americans succeed in building the canal?

Webbing Interrelated Words

Complete the following projects in your notebook or on large chart paper.

1. Create a web of words that begin with the prefix *inter-*. Write *inter-* and its meanings in the center of the web. Record words with the prefix at the ends of spokes extending from the center. On the web, include a definition of each word and a sample sentence. Start with words from this lesson. Use a dictionary to locate others.

2. Create a second word web based on the prefix *circum-*.

3. In the selection are two new words that start with *trans-*. Add those words to the web you made in Lesson 16. Be sure to include the definition of the two words you add and a sample sentence for each.

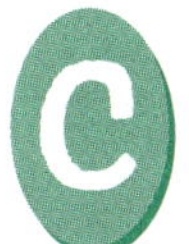

Researching Word Interconnections and Derivations

Work with a partner or two to complete these projects.

1. To excavate for the Panama Canal, the builders first had to blast out solid rock and then dig it away to form a deep trench called the Gaillard Cut. Check a dictionary for the meanings as well as the derivations of *excavate* and *trench*. Write your findings in your notebook. See if you can find other related words to list and define.

2. The Americans used insecticides to help eradicate mosquitoes in the Canal Zone. Check the meanings, uses, and derivation of *eradicate* and *insecticides* in an advanced dictionary. In your notebook, chart your findings for the two words. Also see if you can identify other words that are related to *eradicate* and *insecticide*.
   Clue: For *eradicate*, check for words that begin with *eras-*; for *insecticide*, brainstorm words that end with *-cide*.

3. What is an isthmus? First check the way *isthmus* is used in the selection. Hypothesize what you think the word means. Then verify your hypothesis by checking a dictionary. Make a labeled sketch of an isthmus and write a model sentence in your notebook.

4. Study maps of North and South America to find the names of the mountains that form the Continental Divide. Record those names in your notebook and explain why *Continental Divide* is an excellent name for this series of mountain ranges.

Reviewing the Lesson Words 

Write an answer to each of the following questions.

1. What does a **lock** in a canal do?

2. How do you make a **trench** in solid rock?

3. Why is Panama called an ***isthmus***?

4. For what purpose are **insecticides** used?

5. What do people do when they **circumnavigate** the world?

6. Your grandfather tells you that he will help you only under certain **circumstances**. What does he mean when he tells you this?

7. A friend tells you that he will try to **circumvent** the normal procedures. What does that person mean when he tells you this?

8. A friend tells you that her mother knows a lot about **international** relations. What does your friend mean by that?

9. What happens when two lines **intersect**?

10. What is true about ideas that are **interconnected**?

11. Where do you travel when you take an **intercontinental** airplane flight?

12. What do you do when you **transit** the Panama Canal?

13. What do you do when you **excavate** a site?

14. What do you do when you **eradicate** a disease?

15. In the United States, where would you have to go to see part of the **Continental Divide**?

Writing Workshop

These men played a part in the building of the Panama Canal: Ferdinand de Lessepts, John Stevens, Colonel William Gorgas, George Washington Goethals, and President Theodore Roosevelt. You can get more information about these pioneers on the Web. Track down information on the Internet or consult an online or hardcover encyclopedia. Consider writing a short report on one or more of these men. You may also want to find out more about Vasco Núñez de Balboa, who was one of the first Europeans to explore the area that is now Panama and to view the Pacific Ocean from the western coast of the Americas.

Reviewing What You Know
Lessons 13—17 Word Connections, Higher-Level Test-Taking Skills, and More Analogies

Making Connections among Words that Share a Common Element

Read each set of words in the first column. In the second column, write down the **element** shared by the words in each row of column one. In the third column, enter the **meaning of that element.**

STRATEGY CENTER

When you are asked to write down your answers in columns, always read the captions, or headings, at the top of the columns so that you give the kind of information wanted.

The Words	The Word Element that the Words Have in Common	The Meaning of the Element
Example: millimeter, milliliter, milligram	mill-	thousand
1. quart, quartet, quarter		
2. bicycle, bicentennial, bilingual		
3. century, bicentennial, tricentennial		
4. university, union, united		
5. triple, triplet, tricentennial		
6. anniversary, annual, bicentennial		
7. decimal, December, decade		

B Webbing Related Words

Study the following words: *misinterpret, irrefutable, nonfunctional, nonessential, unable, unacceptable, indifferent, disproportionate, misstep, misdirect, disability, incredible, irregular, irresponsible, nonproductive, disagree, disabled, uncertain, misconception, misinterpret,* and *unnecessary*. Decide which words belong together because they share a similar prefix. Then make a large web with the word *prefixes* at the center. On your web, group related words together. You can add other related words to your visual. Organize your visual in your vocabulary notebook.

C Thinking of Related Words

Complete the following table. Circle the prefixes on the words in the first column. In the second column, write the meaning of the prefix you circled in the first column. In the third column, write down two other words with the same prefix. You can use a dictionary to help you.

The Words	The Meaning of the Prefix	Two Words with the Same Prefix
1. transmit		
2. prevalent		
3. postpone (Make sure your sample words have the same meaning as the prefix on this word.)		
4. circumstance		
5. interconnection		

Using Context Clues to Decide which Word Fits Best.

Find the best word or group of words to complete the sentence. Then fill in the circle next to your answer.

STRATEGY CENTER

Read the sentence. Then read each possible answer and review the meaning of each one. Ask yourself, "Which answer makes the most sense in this context?" Cross out the answers you know for sure are wrong. Then fill in the circle next to the answer that makes the most sense.

1. July 4, 1776, was the birthday of the United States. On July 4, 1976, the nation celebrated its ________________.

   Ⓐ annual anniversary

   Ⓑ bicentennial

   Ⓒ centennial

   Ⓓ tricentennial, or tercentennial

2. Panama is a narrow strip of land that connects two larger landmasses. We call this kind of interconnecting strip an ________________.

   Ⓐ inlet

   Ⓑ island

   Ⓒ islet

   Ⓓ isthmus

3. The groundhog ________________ a burrow in the ground to make a home for herself and her family.

   Ⓐ contracted

   Ⓑ eradicated

   Ⓒ excavated

   Ⓓ transferred

4. Many people shared the ________________ that yellow fever is transmitted on air currents.

Ⓐ conception

Ⓑ misconception

Ⓒ addition

Ⓓ question

5. People who study how languages work and how words are derived are called ________________.

Ⓐ circumnavigators

Ⓑ components

Ⓒ international students

Ⓓ linguists

6. Scientists make preliminary notes in their research notebooks ________________.

Ⓐ very early in their investigations

Ⓑ at an intermediate point in their investigations

Ⓒ at the end of their investigations

Ⓓ many years after finishing their investigations

7. It took the workers five hours to load the ________________ aboard the ship.

Ⓐ cargo Ⓑ isthmus Ⓒ posterity Ⓓ quarantine

8. To prevent the spread of mosquitoes, the scientists sprayed the swamp with ________________.

Ⓐ preconceptions Ⓑ misconceptions Ⓒ insecticides Ⓓ intersections

Using Context Clues to Define Words

Find the word or group of words that best defines the highlighted word. Then fill in the circle next to your answer. Use this strategy:

STRATEGY CENTER

Read the sentence. Then read each answer and try to substitute each answer in place of the highlighted word. Ask, "Which answer best fits here?" Cross out the answers you know for sure are wrong. Then fill in the circle next to the answer that fits best.

1. Dr. Jonas Salk made a great contribution to **posterity** when he developed a vaccine to protect people from the crippling disease of polio.

   Ⓐ future generations

   Ⓑ notes made after an investigation

   Ⓒ medicine taken after a meal

   Ⓓ my own life

2. We crossed the **Continental Divide** when we drove from New York to Los Angeles.

   Ⓐ the isthmus of Panama

   Ⓑ a trench between continents

   Ⓒ a big mountain range

   Ⓓ a series of canal locks

3. The accident happened where two major highways **intersect**.

   Ⓐ go from four lanes to two lanes

   Ⓑ are in need of repairs

   Ⓒ are being repaired

   Ⓓ cross one another

4. My father dug a **trench** so that the water collecting in our yard could run off.

Ⓐ a lock

Ⓑ a dam

Ⓒ a big canal

Ⓓ a ditch

5. Yellow fever was **prevalent** in Cuba in the late 1800s.

Ⓐ illegal

Ⓑ everywhere

Ⓒ unessential

Ⓓ misdirected

6. The prisoners of war experienced many **indignities** after they were captured.

Ⓐ situations in which they felt productive

Ⓑ situations in which they felt disabled

Ⓒ situations in which they felt nonproductive

Ⓓ situations in which they felt disrespected—felt like "nobody"

7. The mariners had to stay **in quarantine** for 40 days.

Ⓐ in prison Ⓑ off by themselves without contact with other people

Ⓒ on an isthmus Ⓓ in a trench

F Recognizing Antonyms

Fill in the circle in front of the word or phrase that has almost the **opposite** meaning of the one given.

STRATEGY CENTER

Think about the meaning of the highlighted word.
Ask, "Which of these other words means almost the opposite?"

1. **credible**

Ⓐ disabled Ⓑ incredible Ⓒ irresponsible Ⓓ unreliable

2. **literate**

Ⓐ able to write Ⓑ able to read Ⓒ illiterate Ⓓ illiteracy

3. **indirect**

Ⓐ different Ⓑ dignified Ⓒ direct Ⓓ doubtful

4. **immense**

Ⓐ disproportional Ⓑ unusual Ⓒ small Ⓓ meaningful

5. **postscript**

Ⓐ note that comes before Ⓑ posterity
Ⓒ misconception Ⓓ note that comes after

6. **rejoiced**

Ⓐ became sad Ⓑ cried out
Ⓒ jumped up and down Ⓓ sang a joyful song

7. **unessential**

Ⓐ necessary Ⓑ nonessential Ⓒ incredible Ⓓ unacceptable

G Completing Analogies

Fill in the circle in front of the answer that best completes each analogy.

STRATEGY CENTER

When you see the symbol of a colon **(:)** in an analogy, say to yourself "is to." When you see the symbol of a double colon **(: :)** in the middle of an analogy, say to yourself "as."

1. **talk turkey** is to **tell it as it is** as **beat around the bush** is to ________________.

   Ⓐ speak indirectly
   Ⓑ pick up fruit that has fallen from a tree
   Ⓒ hit a small tree with a car
   Ⓓ run in circles

2. **blow a fuse : get really mad : : take a powder :** ________________.

   Ⓐ go to the powder room
   Ⓑ powder one's nose
   Ⓒ sprinkle powder on the ground
   Ⓓ run away

3. **take it on the chin : be strong when you are defeated : : talk through your hat :** ________________.

   Ⓐ hold your hat over your mouth while you speak
   Ⓑ make holes in your hat while you speak
   Ⓒ speak without much knowledge
   Ⓓ put your hat on your chin

4. **take a leaf out of your book : follow your example : : strike while the iron is hot :** ________________.

   Ⓐ iron your clothes
   Ⓑ keep your iron hot
   Ⓒ take advantage of an opportunity when it strikes
   Ⓓ go on strike

Part 4

Spanish Words and Words from New Latin

Understanding Formal and Informal Uses of Words

Read this travelogue to learn about things to see and do in the American Southwest. A travelogue tells about a place that people enjoy visiting. Also look for interesting Spanish or new-Latin words that have become part of the English language in recent times. English has borrowed these words directly from the Spanish language and from new Latin, a modern-day version of the Latin language.

A Travelogue about the American Southwest

The American Southwest is a spectacular region of the United States. The Southwest is filled with marvelous **vistas**, or views, of the land in all directions. It also offers fabulous things to do.

First, let us consider the scenery. Cross into Arizona to visit the Grand **Canyon**, a deep gorge that the Colorado River has cut into the earth. There you can see layer upon layer of rocks in many hues of red, orange, pink, brown, and yellow. In the same region, there are **mesas**—high, flat-topped areas. Mesas are like tables of land standing high above the surrounding areas. (In Spanish, *mesa* means "table.") This is an arid region that gets little rainfall. Cacti, yucca, and other plants with fleshy, thick leaves are the main **flora**. It is home to different **fauna**—animals such as Gila monsters, snakes, lizards, tortoises, mice, and small ground squirrels and jackrabbits. These kinds of animals do not need too much water. Most are nocturnal; the animals stay in their cool burrows during the daytime when it is hot and come out at dusk.

In some areas, you will see **haciendas**, large, Mexican-style farmhouses on ranches or estates where wealthier people live. You will also see smaller **adobe** houses made from sun-dried clay bricks. Both the haciendas and the adobe homes are built in the Spanish style. They have thick walls to keep the rooms cool and few windows on the southern sides of the houses.

The towns are constructed in the Spanish style, too. They have a central **plaza** with buildings surrounding an open square as in a quadrangle. If you are lucky when you visit a town, you might drop in on a **fiesta**, a holiday celebration or festival. This is a joyous time when people come together to celebrate and have fun. You might also see people who are dressed up for the fiesta and are wearing **sombreros** (broad-brimmed hats), **ponchos** (cloaks made from large pieces of cloth that have a slit in the middle for the head), or **serapes** (blanket-like shawls in bright shades of red, blue, yellow, and green).

As for entertainment, you might decide to take in a **rodeo**. A rodeo is a show in which cowboys and cowgirls compete to see who can best swing a **lasso** (a kind of rope with a loop, or noose, on the end, used to catch fast horses and cows). They also compete to see who can stay on a bucking **bronco** the longest. A bronco is a partly tamed horse that jumps violently around to try to throw its rider off. At some point during the rodeo, there might be a parade; the cowboys and cowgirls ride their **pintos, palominos,** and other kinds of horses around the arena where the rodeo is being held.

By now you will be hungry. You will want to **mosey** along to a local café—walking over there slowly without rushing. On the menu, you may find barbecued ribs, chili, and tortillas. These Mexican dishes are known by their Spanish names. Barbecued ribs are meaty rib bones that are covered in a spicy tomato sauce. Ribs are generally cooked on a grill. **Chili con carne** is a dish of meat and beans. **Tortillas** are flat, round corn cakes. When you sit down in front of a plate filled with these kinds of foods, you will probably eat them **pronto**. You will want to eat them quickly while they are still warm. If you sit too long at your table in the café, however, someone may feel like telling you to **vamoose**, to get out of there. The food is so great that someone else may want to use your table.

Hopefully, you will be able to visit the American Southwest some day. You will love the scenery, the flora and fauna, the fiestas, the rodeos, and the food. As people say when they put a plateful of food in front of you in a Spanish restaurant, *desfrute*, "enjoy."

Thinking about Ideas and Relationships

1. What kinds of vistas would you expect to see in the southwestern United States? Give more than one example because the question asks for *kinds* of vistas (plural).

2. What kinds of events would you expect to see at a rodeo?

3. What kinds of houses would you expect to see in the Southwest?

4. What kinds of foods would you expect to eat in the Southwest?

Understanding Words from New Latin

The words *vista, flora,* and *fauna* come from New Latin. Use context clues to give the meanings of the words. Remember also the meaning of the Latin root *vis-*.

1. A **vista** is ______________________________.
2. The **flora** of a region are its ______________________________.
3. The **fauna** of a region are its ______________________________.

Understanding Words from Spanish—Thinking about Similarities and Differences

These Spanish words have become part of the English language: *canyon, mesa, hacienda, adobe, fiesta, plaza, sombrero, poncho, serape, rodeo, lasso, bronco, pinto, palomino, chili con carne,* and *tortillas*. Use context clues to answer these questions about the words.

1. What is the difference between a **canyon** and a **mesa**?

2. What is the difference between a **hacienda** and an **adobe** house?

3. What is the difference between a **fiesta** and a **rodeo**?

4. In what way are **ponchos, serapes,** and **sombreros** the same? How do they differ?

5. How are **pintos** and **palominos** the same?

6. How does a **bronco** differ from the kind of horse a person normally rides?

7. How is a **plaza** like a quadrangle?

8. How are **chili** and **tortillas** the same? How are they different?

9. How is a **lasso** different from an ordinary piece of rope?

D Informal Use of Language

The words *mosey, vamoose,* and *pronto* are used only in informal conversation. You would not use them in a report that you are writing. These three words also come to us from the Spanish language. Use context clues to answer these questions. Fill in the circle in front of the answer that best fills each sentence blank.

1. When you **mosey** along to a local café, you ________________.

   Ⓐ walk at a regular speed
   Ⓑ walk slowly without rushing
   Ⓒ vamoose
   Ⓓ rush over there

2. When my neighbor told me to **vamoose**, he meant that I should ______________.

   Ⓐ get out of there fast
   Ⓑ mosey along
   Ⓒ wait for someone to take me in a van
   Ⓓ study the fauna such as moose and deer

3. When Mark's mom told him to come home **pronto** after school, she meant that he should ________________.

   Ⓐ mosey along
   Ⓑ come home quickly
   Ⓒ come home by pinto horse
   Ⓓ come home by the bus labeled *pronto*

E Reviewing the New Words and Expressions

Write the letter of the definition on the line in front of the correct word.

Group One: Nouns

___ 1. fauna	a. views of the land in all directions
___ 2. flora	b. a written description of your travels
___ 3. vistas	c. plants
___ 4. travelogue	d. animals

Group Two: Nouns

___ 5. canyon	e. a large house on a ranch or estate
___ 6. mesa	f. a gorge
___ 7. hacienda	g. a high, flat-topped area generally found in the southwestern United States
___ 8. adobe	h. a quadrangle

___ 9. plaza — i. a holiday-type celebration, especially one held in the southwest

___ 10. fiesta — j. a brick made of sun-dried clay and straw

Group Three: More Nouns

___ 11. sombrero — k. kinds of horses

___ 12. poncho — l. a blanket-like shawl

___ 13. serape — m. a cloak made from a large piece of cloth that has a slit down the middle for the head

___ 14. pinto and palomino — n. kinds of foods

___ 15. chili and tortilla — o. a wide-brimmed hat, especially of the kind worn in the southwestern United States and Mexico

Group Four: Nouns and Verbs

___ 16. rodeo — p. a rope with a loop at the end

___ 17. lasso — q. a partly trained horse that usually bucks when someone tries to ride it

___ 18. bronco — r. a competition among cowboys and cowgirls

___ 19. vamoose — s. right away

___ 20. pronto — t. to get out of a place quickly

___ 21. mosey — u. to move along slowly

F Writing Workshop

Pick a part of the world where you would like to go. Read about that place in an encyclopedia. Take notes grouped under these five topics:

- the kinds of vistas you could see
- the kinds of fauna and flora you could find
- the kinds of houses you could find there
- the kinds of entertainment you might enjoy there
- the kinds of foods you might eat

Then write a short travelogue. Write each paragraph based on a single topic. Use the topics listed above as an outline and the selection on pages 142–143 as a model.

Words from French
Distinguishing between Formal and Informal Use of Language

In the previous lesson, you learned about words that have come into the English language directly from Spanish. In this lesson are many words of French origin. Read the selection to find out how a fine, or excellent, restaurant differs from a fast-food eatery.

A Special Evening Out on the Town

When you think about going out to eat, you probably think about dropping into a fast-food restaurant or visiting the food court at the local mall. Eating out may even bring to mind eating in the school cafeteria rather than at home.

But suppose that one afternoon you receive a written invitation from your great-aunt, who will soon be visiting from France. She invites you to dine out with her at a very expensive and fancy restaurant. At the bottom of your formal invitation are the letters **RSVP**. You know that ASAP means "as soon as possible," but what does RSVP mean?

Actually, RSVP is an abbreviation for a French phrase—**Répondez s'il vous plait**. In English, this phrase means "respond (or answer) if you please." Reading this abbreviation at the end of an invitation, you must sit right down (ASAP) and write a note to your hostess, the person who invited you.

When you and your great-aunt arrive at the restaurant, you notice the beautiful **décor** right away. The place is very classy, decorated to look like it is in Paris. The **maître d'**, or headwaiter, meets you at the door and escorts you and your hostess to your table. After showing you to your table, the maître d' hands you a menu.

Immediately, your great-aunt announces, "You have **carte blanche**. You can order anything you want." You look down, however, and see such words as **soup du jour, entrée, table d'hôte, à la carte,** and **à la mode**. These are French words, and are actually rather easy to understand once you get the hang of it. The *soup du jour* is the special soup of the day, whatever the **chef** has decided to cook that day. The *entrée* is the main course—usually a meat, fish, or pasta dish. *Table d'hôte* refers to a complete dinner that is offered at a set price and includes soup or salad, entrée, and dessert. The French phrase *à la carte* means that you choose each item you want, and you pay for each menu item separately. And *à la mode* generally means served with ice cream. The French phrase *à la mode* literally means "in the style of" or "fashionable." Someone must have decided that having ice cream with your pie was a stylish way to eat it!

Just then a waiter approaches your table and announces, "The soup du jour is pumpkin **bisque**. Our bisque is a rich, creamy soup. I also recommend the **filet mignon** for your entrée tonight. The steak is very tender, a choice cut of beef. Or perhaps you might want something from the **rotisserie**. We slow-roast our chickens over the grill; the chickens turn on a spit for more than an hour so the meat is done to perfection. We also offer a **buffet** from which you can choose what you want and eat as much as you like."

Now you know what you are going to order. Rather than ordering something you do not recognize, you ask for the filet mignon. The steak sounds good, and you do not want to make a **faux pas**. You do not want to make a mistake by ordering something you don't like and will leave on your plate. You want to appear as if you are a food **connoisseur**—a real expert who knows a lot about foods.

The waiter brings your entrée, clears the table when you have finished eating, and hands you the dessert menu. He recommends the **crêpes** or a few **petit fours**. At this point, your hostess explains that *crêpes* are thin French pancakes. Here they are served *á la mode* with a hot fruit sauce as well as with ice cream. *Petit fours* are small, fancy cakes decorated with colorful icing. Since your hostess has given you carte blanche, you order both.

After dessert, you and your great-aunt attend the **ballet**. A ballet is a musical stage show in which the dancers perform in a formal, elegant way. At the end, the audience claps, and someone throws a **bouquet** of flowers on stage as a gift to a dancer. When you leave the ballet, you say, "Thank you," to your hostess. Somehow you remember that *merci* means "thank you" in French, so you add, "*Merci*." When you get home, you write a thank-you note to your great-aunt. On the card, you write, "*Merci*."

Thinking about Ideas and Relationships

1. How is dining in a fine restaurant different from eating out in a fast-food eatery?

2. Posted outside a fine restaurant is the following menu:

Table d'hôte Menu (22 dollars)

Soup du jour: tomato bisque

Entrée: rotisserie chicken

Dessert: strawberry pie à la mode

Explain the menu in "plain English."

Thinking about Words that End with the Letters *-et*

Fill in the circle in front of the word that best fits in the blank.

1. After eating our dinner in a fine French restaurant, we went to the ____________.

   Ⓐ bouquet Ⓑ buffet Ⓒ ballet Ⓓ filet

2. There was a long line at the ____________, so we decided to order the table d'hôte menu rather than serving ourselves.

   Ⓐ bouquet Ⓑ buffet Ⓒ ballet Ⓓ filet

3. I usually order a ____________ because I like tender steak.

   Ⓐ bouquet Ⓑ buffet Ⓒ ballet Ⓓ filet

4. My friend sent me a ____________ for my birthday because she knows I love flowers.

   Ⓐ bouquet Ⓑ buffet Ⓒ ballet Ⓓ filet

In your notebook make a web of French words that end with the letters *-et*. These *-et* words are all pronounced with a long *-a* sound. Start with the four *-et* words in this activity and gradually add others as you think of them.

STRATEGY CENTER

Remember that in French the long *-a* sound is sometimes spelled with the letters *-et* when that sound comes at the end of a word. Examples are the names of the French artists Monet and Manet and the word *beret*, a soft, round hat worn tilted to the side of the head.

Relating French and English Words

Circle the English word next to each French word that is most closely related to the French one. Seeing English words you know in French words you read can help you figure out their meanings. Also check context clues in the selection to help you.

1. décor	decorate	decide	deck	courage
2. répondez	repel	read	respond	doze
3. rotisserie	rat	ranch	roast	Rome
4. plait	please	plan	eat	play

Defining Words Based on Context

Write the letter of the definition on the line in front of the correct word. Check to see how each word is used in the context of the selection.

Group One

____ 1. RSVP	a. the soup of the day, whatever the chef has decided to cook that day
____ 2. maitre d'	b. the headwaiter
____ 3. carte blanche	c. the way a home, restaurant, or shop is decorated
____ 4. soup du jour	d. a free hand; freedom and authority to do what one wants
____ 5. décor	e. the cook
____ 6. chef	f. please answer

Group Two

____ 7. entrée — g. a choice cut of steak

____ 8. bisque — h. with ice cream

____ 9. crêpes — i. thin pancakes

____ 10. à la carte — j. each menu item priced separately

____ 11. à la mode — k. the main course, such as a meat, fish, or pasta dish

____ 12. filet mignon — l. a creamy, rich soup

____ 13. connoisseur — m. an expert in an area such as food or art

Group Three

____ 14. petit fours — n. an arrangement of cut flowers

____ 15. faux pas — o. little cakes with sweet icing

____ 16. table d'hôte — p. a complete meal served at a stated price

____ 17. rotisserie — q. a formal, graceful dance performed to music

____ 18. ballet — r. a mistake or slip up

____ 19. bouquet — s. a gadget with a spit used to roast meat

Relating Words to Their Definitions

1. Complete the crossword puzzle based on the clues. Choose from these words: *à la carte, à la mode, ballet, bisque, bouquet, buffet, carte blanche, chef, crêpes, décor, entrée, faux pas, filet mignon, maitre d', petit fours, rotisserie, RSVP, soup du jour,* and *table d'hôte.*

CLUES

Across

1. a complete meal, offered at a stated price
5. a choice cut of steak
6. an arrangement of many kinds of foods from which to choose
8. decorations
9. please send an answer
11. with ice cream
14. a formal, graceful kind of dance
15. given a free hand
17. a gadget with a spit for cooking meat
18. an arrangement of cut flowers

Down

2. a rich, creamy soup
3. small cakes with icing
4. with a stated price for each menu item ordered
7. an embarrassing mistake
10. the soup of the day
12. headwaiter
13. thin pancakes
15. the chief cook, especially in a fine restaurant
16. the main course of a meal

2. Use the word *connoisseur* in a sentence that has a clear context clue.

F Writing Workshop

Paris, the capital of France, is a beautiful city to visit. Interesting places to see there are the Eiffel Tower, the Arc de Triomphe, and Notre Dame Cathedral. Go to the library and find some books on Paris and its landmarks. Then, during workshop, you may want to write a travelogue and describe some of these famous places.

The Prefixes Super- and Sub- and the Base Words Marine and Aqua

Reviewing Context Clues

Listen to find out about the biggest environmental **catastrophe** in American history. As you think about this disaster, ask yourself, "What personal lessons can I learn from this terrible event?"

Oil Spill in Alaska!

The time was 12:04 AM. The date was Friday, March 24, 1989. The place was Port Valdez. Port Valdez is a seaport on the southern coast of Alaska at the end of the pipeline that carries oil from the interior of Alaska to the coast.

The *Exxon Valdez*, a **supertanker** the length of three football fields, had just taken on its cargo of crude oil from the ship **terminal** located in the port—about 53 million gallons of **unrefined** oil. The terminal, the place where ships dock, is located at the end of a long channel. The channel leads into Prince William Sound. The sound is an area of **supreme**, or very great, natural beauty. Unfortunately, navigating the channel into Prince William Sound is not easy, especially in the dark. It requires an experienced, clear-headed captain who knows how to chart a safe route through a narrow waterway.

Unfortunately, too, the chief **mariner** aboard the huge oil-carrying ship—the captain—had partied the evening before. When the captain boarded his ship, he turned over the **supervision** of the outbound trip to a junior officer. But the younger seaman was not up to overseeing, or directing, the operation. Because of his inexperience, his work was **substandard**. The result was a **catastrophe**—a horrible disaster.

On the way out of the port, the supertanker hit a **submerged** reef. The reef, which was located below the surface of the sea, tore open the **substructure** of the ship, or its lower section. Before the seamen could take any action, gallons of thick black oil from the cargo tanks **spewed** into Prince William Sound just like molten lava gushes from a volcano.

Clean-up crews went into action. To prevent the oil from spreading, they encircled the spill and the *Exxon Valdez* with large, lasso-like collars. They sprayed chemicals on the oil slick to break up the oil into smaller clumps. They went to work to save the **aquatic** animals that lived in the water—playful sea otters and seals, marine birds, whales, fish, and a variety of other animals that live near or in the sea. Sadly, however, the seas in the sound got rough. At one point the clean-up crews had to stop their work until the seas calmed down and the waves **subsided**.

The **marine biologists** knew that this oil spill would have a deadly effect on the fauna and the flora that lived there. And that's what happened, despite the **superhuman** efforts of the scientists who were experts in marine life. It happened despite the fact that many people spent many hours trying to lessen the damage. Many animals died from the **toxic** (or death-causing) substances in the oil. Oil coated the feathers of birds, affecting their ability to keep warm and to fly. Oil covered the fur of sea otters and seals, too. Killer whales died from eating now-toxic, smaller fish on which they normally **subsist**—on which they normally live. The coastline was coated with oil that killed some of the plants found there.

To get an idea of the damage caused by the spill, **superimpose** a map of the part of Alaska affected by the spill over a map of the East Coast of the United States. If you put a map of Alaska on top of a map of the East Coast, you will find that the spill covered an area as large as that between Massachusetts and the Carolinas! You can imagine how many animals were killed or harmed.

What does this mammoth catastrophe say to you and me? To answer this question, think about the responsibilities that go with having an important job. Think also about the effects that a personal failure like this can have on other people and on the fauna and flora of the world.

A Thinking about Ideas and Relationships

How could the catastrophe in Port Valdez have been prevented? Write a short paragraph in your notebook explaining how. Start with a sentence or two in which you summarize the basic facts related to the disaster. Then explain how the catastrophe could have been prevented.

Seeing Word Interrelationships—Basic Prefixes and Roots

1. The prefix *sub-* means "below, under, beneath, almost." For example, a submarine is a ship that travels beneath the sea. In your notebook, make a tower of at least seven words that begin with *sub-*. Next to each, write its meaning. The first two are done as examples. Hint: Check the selection and the dictionary for *sub-* words to list.

sub	marine	a ship that travels beneath the sea
sub	human	beneath the level expected of human beings

2. The prefix *super-* means "over and above; more or greater than what is the norm." For example, a *superhighway* is a highway that is wider than a regular highway. Something that is *supercharged* is really charged up; it is more highly charged than the norm. *Super* also means "going beyond what is expected." For example, a *superhuman* effort is an effort beyond what could be expected of someone. In your notebook, make a tower of at least seven words that begin with *super-*. Next to each word, write the meaning. The first two are done as examples.

super	highway	a broad highway that has six lanes or more
super	market	a big store

3. Words that are built from the base word *marine* have something to do with the sea. For example, a submarine travels under the sea. In your notebook, make a tower of at least five words built from the base word *marine*. Next to each, write the meaning. The first two are done as examples. Mine the dictionary for words to list.

sub	marine	a ship that can travel under the sea
	marine	related to the sea

4. Words that are built from the base word *aqua* have something to do with water. For example, the word *aqua* in English means "water or a bluish-green color like that of water." In your notebook, make a tower of at least five words that are built from the base word *aqua*. Next to each, write the meaning. The first two are done as examples. Use a dictionary to find more words.

aqua		water, or a bluish-green color
aqua	marine	a blue-green colored gemstone

STRATEGY CENTER

When you see a word that begins with the prefix *super-*, relate the word to the idea of "above and over," "greater or more than what is normal," or "beyond what is expected." When you see a word that begins with the prefix *sub-*, relate it to the idea of "under or beneath." Words built from the base word *marine* generally have something to do with the sea. Words built from the base word *aqua* generally have something to do with water.

Finding Context Clues

Next to each highlighted word or phrase below, write a word or phrase from the selection that provides a clue to its meaning. The first three are done as examples.

1. catastrophe: *disaster* ______
2. marine: *sea* ______
3. spewed: *like molten lava gushes from a volcano* ______
4. unrefined: ______
5. the chief mariner: ______
6. toxic: ______
7. supreme: ______
8. supertanker: ______
9. substandard work: ______
10. marine biologists: ______
11. substructure: ______
12. the terminal: ______
13. aquatic animals: ______
14. subsist on: ______
15. submerged: ______

16. supervision: ______________________

17. subsided: ________________________

18. superhuman: _______________________________

19 superimpose: __________________________

Listening for Meaning—Writing from Dictation

Your teacher is going to dictate some sentences and leave out some words. He or she will say the word *blank* in place of the missing word. Listen and decide which word or phrase from those listed here best fits in each sentence blank. In your notebook, write down each sentence with the correct word from the list.

Group 1 Words: catastrophe, mariner, substandard, submerged, substructure, supervised

Group 2 Words: aquatic, marine biologists, spew, superhuman, toxic, unrefined

Group 3 Words: marine, subside, subsist, superimpose, supertankers, supreme, terminal (as a noun)

E Writing Workshop

The world has experienced many natural and manmade disasters. Some well-known examples of natural disasters are the eruptions of Mt. St. Helens in the state of Washington in 1980 and of Mt. Vesuvius in Italy in 79 AD, the great 1906 earthquake and fire in San Francisco, Hurricane Andrew that struck Florida in the twentieth century, and the tsunami—the great tidal wave—that hit in the Far East in December, 2004. Similarly, you know of such manmade catastrophes as those related to the space program (*Apollo 1* and *The Challenger*), the sinking of the *SS Titanic*, and terrorism. Learn more about a catastrophe by accessing the Internet. Then consider writing a brief report similar to the one that opens this lesson. You may want to use the same strategy for your opening paragraph—beginning with the time, date, and place.

The Prefixes Pro-, Anti-, Contra-/Counter-, and Multi-

Grouping Words Based on Prefixes

Read this article to discover why Dr. Norman Borlaug was awarded the Nobel Peace Prize. Ask yourself, "What can I learn from this noted man's life that I can apply to my own life?"

Nobel Prize Winner Norman Borlaug

In December 1970, newspaper headlines announced, "American Norman Borlaug Is Awarded the Nobel Peace Prize!" Who is Norman Borlaug? What did he do that was **pro-peace** and anti-war? What did he do to earn one of the greatest awards in the world—the **Nobel Peace Prize**?

To earn this award, a person or an organization must do something to **promote**, or bring about, world peace. Dr. Norman Borlaug received the Nobel Peace Prize because of his efforts to eradicate hunger in the world. Borlaug is an agricultural scientist. He had spent much of his life until 1970 working on ways to increase food **production**—what is produced, or grown, per acre of land.

Borlaug and the scientists who worked with him decided to try to increase food production because of the hunger they saw around the world. How could they prevent so many people from starving? Borlaug hypothesized that it was important to promote productive **techniques**, or approaches, to farming the land. It was also important to discover new kinds of seeds that **yielded**, or produced, bigger and better crops.

Borlaug turned his attention to the problems of Mexican farmers who were **toiling** long, hard hours in their fields to produce wheat. Although they were farming many acres of land, their farms did not yield enough wheat to feed the Mexican people. Working for more than twenty years, Borlaug and his fellow scientists developed high-yielding wheat seeds. These seeds produced wheat plants that could resist some plant pests and diseases. When the Mexican farmers planted the seeds that Dr. Borlaug had developed, the land yielded two to three times more wheat than before. It was a real miracle—something so **extraordinary** that it was beyond belief!

Dr. Borlaug expanded the program to make it **multinational**. He worked with farmers in India and Pakistan to help them **counteract** many problems they were having with wheat production. The farmers had a **multitude** of agricultural problems—pests, diseases, and poor seeds. They had to **proceed**, or go forward, carefully. They did not want to do anything that would be **counterproductive**—that would produce worse yields than those they were already getting. The farmers probably had little hope that a group of American scientists could help them. **Contrary** to what was expected, the farmers of India and Pakistan overcame some of their problems. They doubled food production over a fifteen-year period by using high-yielding seeds and new **technology**. By technology, we mean new ways of doing things and up-to-date machinery and tools.

This was the beginning of the Green Revolution—a **revolutionary** change in farming technology. In the 1980s and 1990s, the Green Revolution spread to China and parts of Africa. It helped farmers toiling there to produce bigger and better crops. Borlaug is called the father of the Green Revolution, just as George Washington is called the father of the American Revolution.

For dedicating his life to helping feed the hungry people of the world, Dr. Norman Borlaug was awarded the Nobel Peace Prize. At first it may seem **contradictory** to award a peace prize to someone who **launched**, or set in motion, a revolution. But there is no **contradiction**. The Green Revolution is not about war but about how farmers work the land. Its goal is to reduce hunger in the world.

A Thinking about Ideas and Relationships

1. Why was Norman Borlaug awarded the Nobel Peace Prize?

2. How does the Green Revolution differ from other revolutions such as the American Revolution?

3. What is your goal for your life? What do you think you will have to do to achieve it?

B Seeing Word Interrelationships

Add words to this web of prefixes: *pro-*, *contra-/counter-*, *multi-*, *extra-*, and *anti-*. You can find some words in the article you read about the Green Revolution. You can find others in a dictionary. Remember to be able to explain the meanings of the words you include.

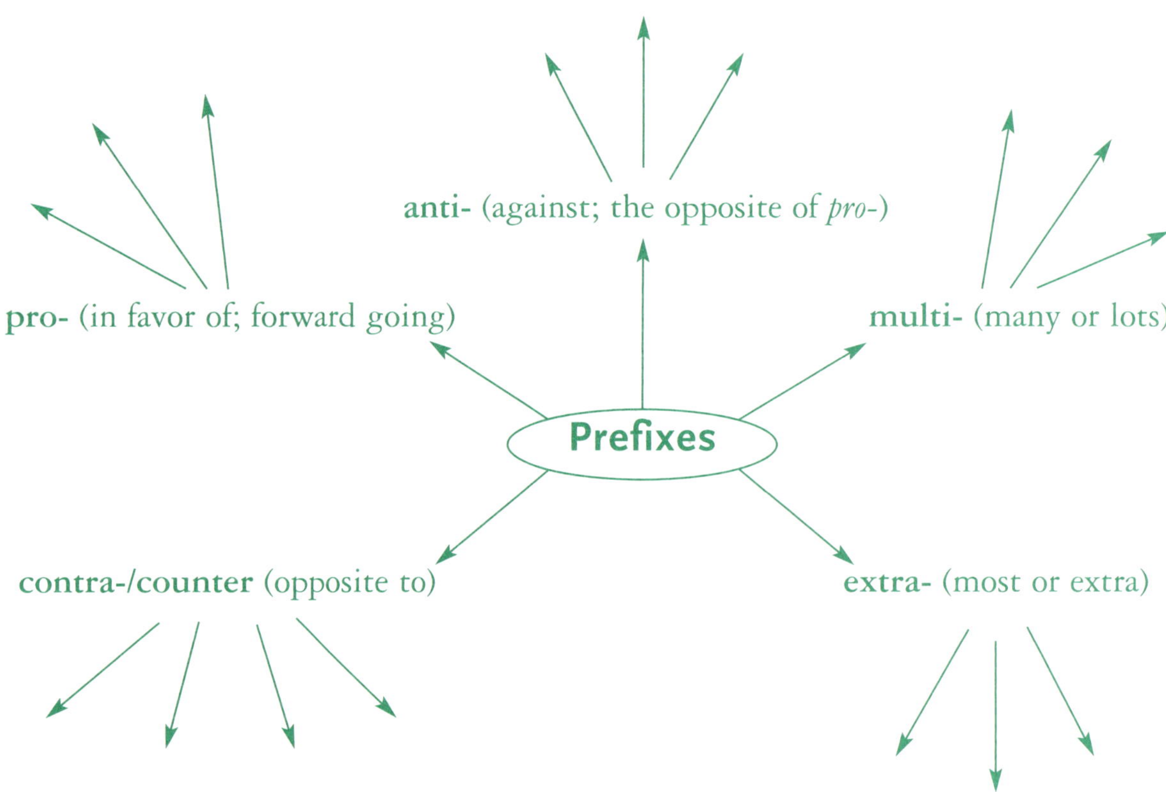

C Defining Highlighted Words

Write the letter of the definition on the line in front of the correct word. Check to see how each word is used in the context of the selection.

Group One: Adjectives

___ 1. extraordinary	a. anti-war
___ 2. multinational	b. beyond the norm; exceptional
___ 3. pro-peace	c. related to or resulting in great change
___ 4. contradictory	d. opposite what has been said or done
___ 5. revolutionary	e. involving many nations
___ 6. counterproductive	f. working against rather than toward a desired goal

Group Two: Verbs

___ 7. to yield	g. to set in motion
___ 8. to launch	h. to work very hard
___ 9. to produce	i. to say that a previous statement is wrong
___ 10. to contradict	j. to make, create, or yield
___ 11. to counteract	k. to bring about, as to bring about peace
___ 12. to proceed	l. to act in a way that overcomes what has happened before
___ 13. to promote	m. to go forward
___ 14. to toil	n. to contribute to or result in

Group Three: Nouns and Other Parts of Speech

___ 15. techniques	o. what is produced, grown, or created
___ 16. technology	p. new scientific ideas and up-to-date machines and gadgets
___ 17. multitude	q. just the opposite of
___ 18. contradiction	r. a statement or idea that proposes the opposite of what has been said
___ 19. contrary to	s. a large number
___ 20. production	t. approaches or methods for doing something

STRATEGY CENTER

Use the idea of "for" to help you understand a word that begins with the prefix *pro-*, and use the idea of "against" to help you figure out the meaning of a word that begins with the prefix *anti-*. Use the idea of "many or lots" to understand a word that begins with the prefix *multi-*, and use the idea of "most or extra" to interpret a word that begins with the prefix *extra-*. Use the idea of "opposite" to help you understand words that start with the prefix *contra-/counter-*.

Using Words in Meaningful Contexts (Cloze)

Write the words where they make the most sense in the sentences.

counteract extraordinary multitude production promoting techniques

1. Norman Borlaug was an ____________ scientist who spent his life trying to increase the food ____________ of the world. He taught farmers to use better agricultural ____________. He helped farmers to ____________ the ____________ of problems they were having related to pests, diseases, and seeds. In doing this, Borlaug was ____________ world peace.

Contrary produce technology yielded

2. ____________ to what the farmers thought would happen, the new ____________ helped them to ____________ bigger and better crops. New machinery and tools as well as new kinds of seeds ____________ more wheat per acre than ever before.

contradiction counterproductive launched multinational proceeded pro-peace revolutionary

3. At first, of course, the scientists ____________ carefully. They did not want to take a chance that the new technology would be ____________. Soon, Borlaug's efforts became ____________. He not only worked with Mexican farmers but with farmers in India, Pakistan, China, and parts of Africa. His results were ____________. They greatly changed the way farmers worked the land. Because of this, we can say that Borlaug ____________ a great revolution.

The Nobel Peace Prize is awarded to people and institutions that are ____________________. Borlaug was involved in a revolution. It was not a ________________________, however, for him to receive the award. Anyone who works to promote greater food production is a hero.

4. Write a sentence using these verbs in the same way they were used in the selection about the Green Revolution.

   Ⓐ toiled

   Ⓑ yielded

   Ⓒ promoted

   Ⓓ proceeded

Writing Workshop

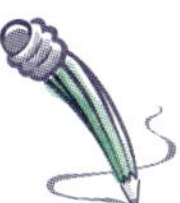

Other exceptional people who have received the Nobel Peace Prize are President Jimmy Carter, President Theodore Roosevelt, President Woodrow Wilson, Mother Theresa, Linus Pauling, Martin Luther King Jr., Jane Addams, and Nelson Mandela. Organizations that have won the prize include the International Red Cross and Doctors without Borders. On the Internet, track down information about one of these people or organizations. Write a brief essay about what the person or organization did to earn the award.

The Suffix -Ment and a Review of Basic Prefixes and Suffixes

Inspiring You to Act for the Good of Others

Listen to this biography of an extraordinary spiritual and political leader from the Asian subcontinent of India. Think, "What made Mahatma Gandhi an **inspirational** leader—a person who encouraged or inspired others to stand up and take positive action?"

Marching Peacefully for Freedom

Mahatma Gandhi was an inspirational leader in India when the **spirit** of reform was in the air. He is known today for his belief in **nonviolent** resistance to unjust laws. He urged his supporters to **resist**, or stand up against, unfair governmental **policies**—unfair rules and regulations. He encouraged the Indian people to use peaceful **disobedience** as a way of gaining independence for their country. He urged them not to give in to **discouragement**. This is what Gandhi said: "Hatred can only be overcome by love."

Gandhi first got involved in **politics**—activities dealing with the government and the state—when he was living in South Africa in the early 1900s. In South Africa, Gandhi struggled to counteract anti-Indian **discrimination**. By discrimination, we mean a different and unjust way of treating people because of their race, religion, or gender.

Returning home to India in 1915, Gandhi was welcomed as a hero because of his anti-discrimination activities in South Africa. The Indian people began to call him "Mahatma," which means "great soul." This was during the First World War. At that time, Gandhi was pro-government, even though the British controlled India. Gandhi supported the British because he believed that when the war was over, Britain would grant India her freedom. This did not happen. Britain reneged on her promise, and something very bad happened instead.

In 1919, government troops fired on unarmed Indians who were protesting the **suppression** of their rights. The British had forbidden any political activity in India that might lead to an independent India. They would not allow public **expressions** of displeasure against the government. They would not allow the Indian people to make any statements containing anti-British ideas. Many Indian people were **massacred** in this cold-blooded attack.

Gandhi now began to preach peaceful noncooperation with the British. He proposed that the Indians not pay the tax that the British had **imposed**, or placed, on salt. In 1930, Gandhi led a 200-mile march to the sea to protest the salt tax. Hundreds of supporters walked with him across India until they reached the sea. There Gandhi and his followers dipped their fingers into the salt that lay on the seashore and put it into their mouths. When they did this, they were **mindful** that this was an illegal act.

Can you believe that such a simple act could be against the law? At that time in India that act was illegal. Even though salt is a staple in everyone's diet, Indians could not use salt or collect it from their own seashores without paying a tax on it—a tax that went to the British-led government.

During the march in 1930, Gandhi reminded his followers that they were not to strike back with force against the British. He gave them encouragement when he said, "True nonviolence is mightier than the mightiest violence."

Gandhi also demanded that the **untouchables** of India be invited to join the march to the sea. The untouchables belonged to the lowest social **caste**, or group, in the country. They did the work no one else would do, and other Indians would not interact with them. Untouchables could not move up in the world regardless of their intelligence or willingness to work hard. Gandhi would not stand for this kind of discrimination and **repression**.

As punishment for leading the salt march, Gandhi was imprisoned. When he was released, Gandhi continued to work for self-rule in India and equal rights for all people. He spent the remainder of his life serving others and living a very simple life. He died in 1948, shot by a religious **fanatic**—a person with extreme beliefs who was disturbed by Gandhi's acceptance of people of different religious faiths.

Thinking about Ideas and Relationships

1. What is nonviolent resistance?

2. What have you learned from the life of Mahatma Gandhi that relates to your own life?

Connecting Words with the Suffix *-Ment*

1. What common element do you see in these words: *discouragement, requirement, enjoyment, enrichment, excitement, amazement, imprisonment,* and *government?*

2. What is the meaning of the suffix found on the words? Which part of speech are these words? Check your dictionary to find out. Write your answers here.

3. In your notebook, make a word tower that highlights the relationships between the prefixes, the base word, and the suffixes on these words: *govern, government, governmental, pro-government, anti-government, ungovernable, governor, governess,* and *governance.*

Seeing Prefixes and Suffixes in Complex Words

In the second column, write the prefixes and/or suffixes you see in the words listed in the first column. In the third column, write the meanings of these elements. In the fourth column, write one or two words built from the same prefix and/or suffix. Two examples show you how to proceed. Refer to a dictionary for the meanings of the prefixes and suffixes and for related words. Note that prefixes may be spelled differently depending on the root to which they are affixed. For instance, *sub-* becomes *sup-* when affixed to the root *port-*, meaning "to carry."

Multisyllabic Words	Prefixes and/or Suffixes	Meanings of Prefixes and/or Suffixes	Other Words with the Prefixes and/or Suffixes
1. supporter	sub-; -er	under; one who	submarine; mariner
2. anti-government	anti-; ment	against; act of or means of	anti-democratic; excitement
3. nonviolent			
4. anti-British			
5. cooperation			
6. illegal			
7. mindful			
8. untouchable			
9. peacefully			
10. leader			
11. return			
12. displeasure			
13. encourage			
14. independent			
15. express			
16. repression			
17. extraordinary			
18. imprisonment			
19. counteract			
20. subcontinent			

D Using Everything You Know about Words

Fill in the circle in front of the word or phrase that best defines the highlighted word or phrase in each sentence. Use context, prefixes, suffixes, and base words as clues.

1. My brother Sam got involved in **politics** just after he graduated from college.

   Ⓐ activities dealing with money

   Ⓑ activities dealing with government and the state

   Ⓒ activities dealing with extraordinary people

   Ⓓ activities dealing with education

2. Congress accepted the **policies** that the president proposed.

   Ⓐ rules and regulations Ⓑ letters Ⓒ organizations Ⓓ laws

3. The government **imposed** a higher income tax on the people of the nation.

   Ⓐ agreed to Ⓑ recommended

   Ⓒ put into place and required Ⓓ thought about

4. The government developed a policy of **suppressing** critical ideas.

   Ⓐ putting down Ⓑ agreeing to Ⓒ considering Ⓓ clarifying

5. The government did not allow any **expressions** of opinion that were anti-governmental.

   Ⓐ ironing out Ⓑ policies Ⓒ mistakes Ⓓ statements

6. **Disobedience** was harshly punished.

   Ⓐ refusal to obey Ⓑ obedience Ⓒ misinformation Ⓓ generosity

7. Those who **resisted** were imprisoned even though their acts were nonviolent.

   Ⓐ massacred others Ⓑ discriminated against others

   Ⓒ spoke up and disobeyed Ⓓ robbed others

8. The **spirit** of reform was in the air.

   Ⓐ uplifting feeling or belief Ⓑ clouds

   Ⓒ discouragement Ⓓ angry feeling

9. At that time many people gave speeches that were **inspirational** and encouraged listeners to take nonviolent action.

Ⓐ scary and short
Ⓑ fanatical and unjust
Ⓒ exciting and uplifting
Ⓓ dull and long

10. At that time many people gave speeches that were inspirational and encouraged listeners to take **nonviolent** action.

Ⓐ very fanatical
Ⓑ discouraging
Ⓒ peaceful
Ⓓ inspirational

11. At that time in India the **caste system** was prevalent. Some people were called untouchables under this discriminatory system.

Ⓐ system of social classes
Ⓑ anti-governmental system
Ⓒ system of free education
Ⓓ system of democracy

12. At that time in India the caste system was very strong. Some people were called **untouchables** under this discriminatory system.

Ⓐ people not allowed to interact with others and considered below other people
Ⓑ people who were considered to be above other people
Ⓒ people who favored nonviolent action
Ⓓ people who could not touch each other

13. Young children were even taught to **discriminate against** the untouchables.

Ⓐ act differently and unjustly toward
Ⓑ act in an exceptionally nice way
Ⓒ infect
Ⓓ inoculate

14. The leaders **were mindful of the fact** that they could be imprisoned for their acts of disobedience.

Ⓐ did not realize
Ⓑ carefully considered the fact
Ⓒ abolished the fact
Ⓓ forgot about the fact

15. During the rebellion, brave people were **massacred** in a cold-blooded attack.

Ⓐ grouped together in a plaza
Ⓑ killed
Ⓒ hurt
Ⓓ rewarded

16. This was part of the government's policy of **repression**.

Ⓐ accepting others
Ⓑ rewarding those who had done well
Ⓒ putting down any criticism
Ⓓ encouraging different points of view

17. Gandhi did not give in to **discouragement**. Instead, he forged ahead with greater determination.

Ⓐ thoughtlessness, or lack of consideration of others
Ⓑ sad feelings, or a sense of hopelessness
Ⓒ determination
Ⓓ hatred, or loathing

18. The man who killed Gandhi was **a fanatic**.

Ⓐ a person with extreme beliefs
Ⓑ a person who loves freedom
Ⓒ a person who believes in political disobedience
Ⓓ a person who believes in discrimination

Writing Sentences with Complex Words

In your notebook, write sentences with these words or phrases: *nonviolent resistance, inspirational book, governmental policies, politics, peaceful disobedience, impose a tax, racial discrimination, cruel suppression, expressions of anti-government feeling, discouragement, massacred, caste system, untouchables, fanatic, mindful of,* and *harsh repression*. Use the sentences in Activity D and in the selection on pages 166–167 as models.

F Writing Workshop

Dr. Martin Luther King Jr. practiced nonviolent resistance to oppose racial discrimination in the United States. Access information about Dr. King on the Internet. Write a brief report explaining how Dr. King and his supporters used nonviolent resistance.

Reviewing What You Know
Lessons 19–23
Skills for Making Word Connections

Seeing Word Interrelationships

Tell how the words on each line are related. Be specific. Give the prefix, suffix, root, base word, or meaning you see in all the words on the line. If possible, also give the meaning or derivation of a shared prefix, root, or base word. The first one has been done as an example. Use a dictionary when you need to.

Group One

1. unrefined, refined

   Unrefined and *refined* are opposites, or antonyms. The prefix *un-* tells that *unrefined* means "not refined or crude." *Refined* means "classy or upscale." Both words are built from the base word *fine*, which means "of a high grade or level."

2. technical, nontechnical

3. catastrophe, disaster

4. interior, exterior

5. anti-American, pro-American

6. plaza, quadrangle, square

Group Two

7. substructure, submarine, subside, substance

8. multimedia, multinational, multitude

9. supervision, superstructure, superintendent, supertanker

10. contradict, counteract, contrary, counterproductive

Group Three

11. marine, mariner, marina, submarine

12. repress, expression, suppression, pressure

13. impose, superimpose, compose, position

14. poncho, rodeo, sombrero, bronco

15. ballet, filet, bouquet, buffet

16. vamoose, mosey, pronto

B Relating Items through Analogies

Fill in the circle in front of the item that best completes the analogy.

Group One

1. plant : flora : : animal : ____________

   (A) whale (B) rose (C) fauna (D) flower

2. beaver : fauna : : rose : ____________

   (A) flora (B) animal (C) word (D) work

3. fiesta : Spanish word : : entrée : ____________

   (A) word (B) French word (C) Greek word (D) Latin word

4. host : hostess : : actor : ____________

   (A) acted (B) acting (C) actress (D) act

5. filet mignon : steak : : tomato bisque : ____________

   (A) entrée (B) soup (C) salad (D) dessert

Group Two

6. refined : classy : : unrefined : ____________

   (A) sugar (B) oil (C) crude (D) fine

7. ASAP : as soon as possible : : RSVP : ____________

   (A) please answer (B) please come

   (C) please come as soon as possible (D) please enjoy

8. marine : sea : : aquatic : ____________

   (A) animal life (B) water (C) green (D) marine

9. super : above : : sub : ____________

   (A) against (B) for (C) over (D) under

10. extraordinary : common : : superb : ____________

    (A) terrible (B) supreme (C) counterproductive (D) multinational

11. pinto : horse : : hacienda : ____________

    (A) car (B) mesa (C) festival (D) house

Relating Words to the Context

Fill in the circle in front of the word or phrase that best fits into the blank.

1. The train pulled into the ______________ and all the passengers disembarked.

   Ⓐ channel Ⓑ vista Ⓒ fanatic Ⓓ terminal

2. We used a bridge to get across the ______________.

   Ⓐ mesa Ⓑ canyon Ⓒ vista Ⓓ plaza

3. The engineers had to develop new ______________ to solve the extraordinary technical problems they faced in cleaning up the oil spill.

   Ⓐ procedures Ⓑ catastrophes Ⓒ suppressions Ⓓ untouchables

4. The school principal developed some new ______________ that told us what we were allowed to do and not to do.

   Ⓐ fanatics Ⓑ contradictions Ⓒ spirits Ⓓ policies

5. When the soldiers opened fire on the crowd, the result was a terrible ______________ in which many citizens died.

   Ⓐ repression Ⓑ massacre Ⓒ expression Ⓓ suppression

6. To earn the Nobel Peace Prize, a person or an organization must make a contribution that ______________ world peace.

   Ⓐ suppresses Ⓑ represses Ⓒ imposes Ⓓ promotes

7. Gandhi was killed by a ______________ who had extreme beliefs about people of different religious faiths.

   Ⓐ fanatic Ⓑ spirit

   Ⓒ pro-Indian Ⓓ anti-war protester

8. Gandhi was mindful of the fact that the ______________ system had existed in India for many centuries. However, Gandhi was against any form of discrimination or repression.

   Ⓐ caste Ⓑ nonviolent resistant

   Ⓒ pro-British Ⓓ democratic political

9. In a democracy, the people should be ______________; they are the ones who should have the greatest power.

   Ⓐ submerged Ⓑ disobedient Ⓒ supreme Ⓓ imprisoned

10. The marine biologists faced a ______________ of problems that they had to counteract if they were to help the sea animals survive.

Ⓐ supertanker Ⓑ spirit Ⓒ spill Ⓓ multitude

11. Martin Luther King Jr. was an ______________ speaker who could make his listeners care deeply about the injustices of discrimination, segregation, and repression.

Ⓐ inspirational Ⓑ unrefined Ⓒ aquatic Ⓓ irritating

Writing Comparisons, Contrasts, and Opinions

In your notebook write four paragraphs in which you tell how the following people are similar to and different from one another: the captain of the *Exxon Valdez*, Norman Borlaug, and Mahatma Gandhi. In your first paragraph, focus on the mariner. Use such words as *catastrophe, supertanker, substructure,* and *submerged* when writing about what he did. In the second paragraph, write about Borlaug. Use such words as *Nobel Peace Prize, production, techniques, revolutionary,* and *promote* when writing about his work. Write about Gandhi in the third paragraph. Use such words as *nonviolent resistance, discrimination, suppression,* and *imposed* when writing about Gandhi's contribution. In your fourth paragraph, tell which of the these men you think was the greatest and which was the weakest. Explain your choice.

Seeing the Wonder of Words

Words are wonderful! You have been studying many words—prefixes, suffixes, and base words. Pick any two that are your favorites. For each, write a paragraph in which you tell about the word and why you think it is wonderful.

For example, one of my favorite words is the word *antidiscrimination*. If I were to write about this word, here are some of the thoughts I would include. I think *antidiscrimination* is a wonderful word because I believe it is wrong to discriminate, or to act differently toward people in an unjust way because of their race, religion, or sex. The word is interesting because it is derived from a Latin word that means "to divide." I like the word because the prefix *anti-* says clearly that I am against discrimination—that I am against dividing people into groups and segregating them from one another.

Here are some words to consider as topics for your paragraphs: *supertanker, substandard, counteract, counterproductive, mesa, lasso, décor,* and *nonviolent*.

Glossary

Explanation

- The guide word at the top of each page tells you which words are found on that page.

- After each entry are letters in parentheses that are marked to show you how to pronounce the word. One kind of mark shows what syllables to stress, or accent, as you pronounce the word. There are two kinds of accents: the primary accent shown in darker type (**ʹ**) and the secondary accent shown in lighter type (ʹ).

- Other marks, called *diacritical marks*, show you how to pronounce the vowel sounds. Here is a guide to how the vowel sounds are shown in this glossary. Next to each marked letter or group of letters are examples of words with that vowel sound.

Pronunciation Guide

ā	base, gate, mane (long *a* sound)
ä	tar, father
ē	me, feet, slowly (long *e* sound)
ī	light, bite, file (long *i* sound)
ō	open, most, boat (long *o* sound)
a	fat, pack, last (short *a* sound)
e	let, gem, dead (short *e* sound)
i	lit, rim, fin (short *i* sound)
o	hot, gone, fox (short *o* sound)
u	up, munch, brunch (short *u* sound)
â	barn, farm
ô	order, long, awkward
ü	rule, statue
û	turn, blur, firm, word
oo	foot, good
o͞o	food, root, new, due, crude
ou	out, mouth
oi	oil, spoil
ə	the first vowel sound in *amaze*
ə	the last vowel sound in *assignment*
ə	the last vowel sound in *pencil*
ə	the last vowel sound in *atom*
ə	the last vowel sound in *cheerful*

abhor (ab hôr´), *verb,* to shrink away with horror or disgust; to hate. Fran and Mike *abhor* hearing about any mistreatment of animals.

accept (ak sept´), *verb,* to take what is offered. Chandra will *accept* Mike's invitation to dinner.

access (ak´ ses), *noun,* admittance; the ability or right to enter or make use of. Because we bought tickets in advance, we were given *access* to the special exhibit.

accidentally (ak´ sə dent´ lē), *adverb,* not on purpose; by chance. Harry *accidentally* broke the window while trying to repair the door.

account (ə kount´), *noun,* an explanation in detail about some event or thing. The teacher gave a lengthy *account* of the causes of the American Revolution.

adobe (ə dō´ bē), *noun,* sun-dried brick. *Adobe* houses are built with bricks made of clay and straw that are dried and hardened by the sun.

afar (ə fär´), *adverb,* from far off. From *afar,* the blinking light was barely visible.

affect (a fekt´), *verb*, to produce a result; to have an influence on. A very low temperature can *affect* the water pipes, causing them to freeze.

à la carte (ä´ lə kärt´), *adverb* and *adjective*, with a separate price for each item on the menu. From the French, the phrase *a la carte* is translated as "by the menu." We ordered from the *à la carte* menu because we did not want a complete dinner.

à la mode (ä´ lə mōd´), *adjective*, served with ice cream. From a French phrase meaning "in the fashion of." We like to eat apple pie *à la mode* with vanilla ice cream.

ambush (am´ bush), *verb*, to make a surprise attack from a hidden position. The thief broke into the bank, but the police were waiting behind the door to *ambush* him.

anniversary (an´ə vûr´ sə rē), *noun*, the yearly return of some special date. The United States celebrated its 200th *anniversary* on July 4, 1976.

annual (an´ yü əl), *adjective*, coming once a year. The graduation ceremony is an *annual* event.

antennae (an ten´ ē), *plural noun* (singular form, *antenna*). 1. devices for sending or receiving electronic waves of energy. The new, taller *antennae* allowed the television station signal to reach more distant places. 2. feelers on the heads of some creatures such as insects and lobsters. A grasshopper has two *antennae*.

apply (ə plī´), *verb*, to ask for. Maya *applied* for a part-time job at a clothing store in the mall.

aquatic (ə kwä´ tik), *adjective*, of or in the water. Fish and ducks are *aquatic* animals.

arch (ärch), *verb*, to bend into a curve. When the cat saw a dog coming down the street, she *arched* her back, lifted her tail, and hissed loudly in warning. *noun*, a curved structure that is designed to carry the weight of something above it. A stone *arch* supported the bridge.

ballet (ba lā´), *noun*, 1. a graceful dance with precision movements. Maria has been studying *ballet* for two years. 2. a dance presentation with music, costumes, and scenery based on a story or theme. Our class went to see the ballet *Swan Lake*.

bank (bangk), *noun*, 1. a place of business for receiving and lending money. Carla deposited her check at the *bank*. 2. a storage place or reserve. My computer has a large memory *bank*. 3. a set of similar items arranged in rows. Music organs have a double row of keys in *banks*. 4. a pile or mass of something. We fell into a snow *bank*.

barrier (bar´ ē ər), *noun*, something blocking or standing in the way. A wooden *barrier* prevented us from driving down that street.

bedraggled (bi drag´əld), *adjective*, wet and limp. Tara got caught in the rain and looked *bedraggled* when she came in with dripping hair and her wet shoes.

befall (bi fôl´), *verb*, to happen to. We don't know what will *befall* them if they insist on entering that dangerous construction area.

behold (bi hōld´), *verb*, to look upon; to see (often used imperatively). *Behold* what you have done!

belittle (bi lit´ l), *verb*, to make little or less important; to depreciate. Harry wasn't doing a good job himself, so he *belittled* the work of the others to try to make himself look better.

berate (bi rāt´), *verb*, to scold. The parents *berated* their child for crossing the street without first looking in both directions.

besmirch (bi smûrch´), *verb*, to soil; to detract from. John did not want his good name *besmirched* by his friend's false account.

bestow (bi stō´), *verb*, to give something as a gift. Dorothy *bestowed* a gift of children's books to the library.

bicentennial (bī´sen ten´ ē əl), *noun*, a 200th anniversary. The United States celebrated its *bicentennial* in 1976.

bisque (bisk), *noun*, a thick soup made from vegetables, meat, or seafood. Lobster *bisque* is a rich creamy soup made with shellfish.

bondage (bon´dij), *noun*, slavery; lack of freedom. There are places in the world where people are still in *bondage* and have lost, or never had, their freedom.

bouquet (bō kā´ or bo͞o kā´), *noun*, a cluster or arrangement of flowers. The *bouquets* we saw at the flower shop were of many sizes, colors, and combinations of beautiful flowers.

breed (brēd), *verb*, 1. to produce young. Fish *breed* in large numbers near the shore of the river near my home. 2. to raise or grow. People who *breed* dogs or other animals carefully choose the male and female animals for desirable traits.

bronco (brong´ kō), *noun*, a partly tamed horse. Horses in western North America that are not fully trained to be ridden are called *broncos*.

buffet (bə fā´), *noun*, 1. a meal where people help themselves to items set out on a long table. The hostess served a *buffet* rather than offering a sit-down meal. 2. a piece of furniture typically found in a dining room. The *buffet* stood at the end of the room and contained china and glassware.

canyon (kan´yən), *noun*, a deep valley that has steep cliffs on each side. The Colorado River runs through the Grand *Canyon*. The river carved out the *canyon* over thousands of years.

cargo (kär´ gō), *noun*, a load of goods carried by ship or plane. The *cargo* was loaded into large metal containers that were lifted up onto the ship.

carte blanche (kärt blänch´), *noun*, complete freedom to do what you want in a certain situation. The expression *carte blanche* comes from the French and means a blank document or card on which you can write your own order. My friend Marta gave me *carte blanche* to pick out books from the library for her.

caste (kast), *noun*, a social class in India, for example, the untouchables. *Castes* have restrictions placed upon them as to what work occupation they may have.

catastrophe (kə tas´ trə fē), *noun*, a terrible disaster. The earthquake that destroyed the village was a major *catastrophe* for those living there.

cause (kôz), *noun*, 1. the purpose or end result for which a person or group strives. Liberty is the *cause* for which people have fought over the centuries. 2. something that produces an effect. The police could not figure out the *cause* of the accident. *verb*, to bring about or to make happen. Eating too much pizza can *cause* indigestion.

charge (chärj), *verb*, 1. to attack; to rush at. The rhino *charged* the lions and frightened them away. 2. to give a task to. My teacher *charged* me with the responsibility of gathering materials for the class project. *noun*, the price or expense. The *charge* for the bus ticket was only seven dollars, which was a very good price for the round-trip fare.

chef (shef), *noun*, a cook or chief cook. Large restaurants have many *chefs*; one may be in charge of salads, another meats, and a third, pastries.

chili (chil´ē), *noun*, a hot pepper; sauce made from the chili pepper. Some chili sauce made with meat is called *chili con carne* because *con carne* in Spanish means "with meat."

circumnavigate (sîr´kəm nav´ə gāt), *verb*, to go around. Ships can sail through the Panama Canal to avoid *circumnavigating* South America.

circumstance (sûr´kəm stans´), *noun*, a condition that affects something else. Two *circumstances*—bad weather and slippery roads —made the principal decide to cancel the game.

circumvent (sûr´ kəm vent´), *verb*, to get around something. Several immoral people tried to *circumvent* the rules by not counting everyone's vote, but the officials caught up with them.

clam up (klam up), *verb*, 1. the action of a clam or other bivalve closing the two halves of its shell together. The bivalve *clammed up* when we dug a hole near it. 2. an expression meaning to keep quiet and not comment or talk about something. When Jim heard the others coming down the hall, he *clammed up* because he did not want them to know his plans.

clever (klev´ər), *adjective*, intelligent, bright; skilled at something. Carmen is very *clever* at learning languages; she is now listening to tapes to teach herself to speak Italian.

companionship (kəm pan´yən ship), *noun*, fellowship. All the group members got along well with each other; they shared true *companionship*.

complex (kəm pleks´), *adjective*, having many parts; hard to understand. The children had trouble following the *complex* directions the principal gave them.

component (kəm pō´nənt), *noun*, a necessary part of something. Cheese is a basic *component* of pizza.

con (kon), *verb*, to swindle or defraud. Con is a clipped form of *confidence* man or *confidence* game. Troy gained our confidence with his friendly manner, but his manner was not genuine; he was actually trying to *con* us out of our money.

connoisseur (kon´ ə sûr´), *noun*, a person with lots of knowledge about art, music, or food. Brady is a true food *connoisseur*; he knows what is good and seeks it out.

connotation (kon´ə tā shən), *noun*, the implied or associated meaning of a word based on the way people feel about the word. From the *connotation* of the words my friend used, I knew that she was not a happy camper.

considerable (kən sid´ər ə bəl), *adjective*, much; a lot. There was a *considerable* amount of work still remaining when the crew left for the day.

Continental Divide (kon´tə nen´təl di vīd´), *noun*, a series of mountain ridges running from Alaska to the southern tip of South America that separates the streams that flow eastward from those that flow westward. The Rocky Mountains are part of the *Continental Divide*.

contract (kən trakt´), *verb*, 1. to shorten or reduce in size. My pupils *contracted* in the bright sunlight. 2. to get; to bring on one's self. The boys *contracted* the measles. *noun*, an official document that sets forth the terms of a legal agreement. The writer had to sign a *contract* that told when she would submit her manuscript to her publisher.

contradiction (kon´trə dik´shən), *noun*, an act of saying the opposite, or contradicting. What you say today is a *contradiction* of what you told us yesterday.

contradictory (kon´trə dik´tə rē), *adjective*, involving a contradiction. His statement was *contradictory* to his principles.

contrary (kon´trer´ ē), *adjective*, different in character; opposite. The directions she gave me to the school were *contrary* to what I saw on the map.

converse (kən vers´), *verb*, to talk together. The friends wanted to *converse* with each other.

corrode (kə rōd´), *verb*, to eat away, especially by chemical action. The iron pipe began to *corrode* after it had been left out in the rain.

council (koun´ səl), *noun*, a group of people elected to govern. Our town *council* elects one of its members to be the mayor of our town.

counsel (koun´ səl), *verb*, to give advice; to advise. The school counselor tries to *counsel* others by recommending courses that they might like to take. *noun*, the *counsel*, or advice that is given. The *counsel* that Herb got helped him to find a job.

counteract (koun´ tər akt´), *verb*, to oppose an action. The noisy students are trying to *counteract* the poor impression they made during the last ball game by behaving well during this one.

counterproductive (koun´tər prə duk´ tiv), *adjective*, hindering rather than advancing a purpose. The committee members were *counterproductive* because they created more problems than solutions.

coward (kou´ ərd), *noun*, a person who lacks courage and becomes fearful easily. Jerry behaves like a *coward* and backs away from any action in which he could possibly fail.

crafty (kraf´ tē), *adjective*, skillful in deceiving others. Teresa was *crafty* in making others think that she knew more about things than they did.

credentials (kri den´shəlz), *noun*, papers such as letters or certificates that show the bearer's right to confidence or authority. Nora's *credentials* showed that she was a certified public accountant.

credit (kred´it), *noun*, an honor or commendation. On school awards day, we give *credit* to those who work hard and achieve worthy goals. *verb*, to give honor to; to regard as having performed an action. We *credit* the principal with developing a new reading program in the school.

crêpes (kräps), *noun*, thin pancakes. My sister enjoys eating *crêpes* rolled up and covered with powdered sugar and orange sauce.

crystal (kris´ tl), *noun*, a solid, mineral substance with flat sides and angles. We saw purple *crystals* of amethyst in the museum that were a gorgeous hue and had sharp edges.

deal **(dēl)**, *verb*, 1. to hand out playing cards. It was Ashkar's turn to *deal* the cards. 2. to do business with. Kayla likes to *deal with* electricians because she was a physics major in college. 3. to handle or consider. I could not *deal with* the way he *dealt* the cards. *noun*, 4. a favorable bargain, I got the best *deal* that I could. 5. an amount, as in "He had a great *deal* of experience."

decade **(dek´ād)**, *noun*, a period of ten years. *Decade* is a word derived from the Greek word *deka*, meaning "ten." We have lived in our house for a *decade*—from 1990 to 1999.

deceive **(di sēv´)**, *verb*, to make a person believe that something false is true. Jack tried to *deceive* the teacher when he told her that his dog had chewed up his homework paper. His deception did not work!

declare **(di klâr´)**, *verb*, to state strongly. The governor *declared* that she had never seen people cooperate as well as they did during the hurricane.

décor **(dā kôr´)**, *noun*, a style of decoration. The room *décor* was in an old-fashioned style.

delectable **(di lək´ tə bəl)**, *adjective*, greatly pleasing; delightful, delicious. We enjoyed a *delectable* treat—an éclair filled with cream and covered with chocolate.

delicate **(del´ i kət)**, *adjective*, fragile, easily damaged or destroyed. *Delicate* items such as crystal glasses need to be handled gently and with care.

denotation **(de´nō tā´ shən)**, *noun*, the meaning of a term or word when it identifies something by naming it. The literal or dictionary definition of a word is that word's *denotation*.

dependent **(di pen´ dənt)**, *adjective*, relying on some person or thing for support or help. Young children are *dependent* on their parents for daily care, food, and shelter.

depressed **(di pressed´)**, *adjective*, downcast, sad, and lonely. Al was *depressed* after his dog died.

deserve **(di zerv´)**, *verb*, to have a right to. Edna was worthy of the award because of her hard work and her skill; she *deserved* it.

disability **(dis´ə bil´ə tē)**, *noun*, a physical or mental condition or limitation that interferes with normal achievement. A guide dog can greatly improve a blind person's quality of life and lessen the impact of his or her *disability*.

discouragement **(di skûr´ ij mənt)**, *noun*, the state of being without hope or confidence. Midway through the long race, Marty felt a sense of *discouragement*, but he did not give up and eventually reached his goal.

discrimination **(di skrim´ə nā´shən)**, *noun*, an act of prejudice. To act with *discrimination* toward someone because of race, religion, or sex is unjust and illegal.

disguise **(dis gīz´)**, verb, to hide one's identity by looking like someone or something else. Actors *disguise* themselves by applying false hair and makeup.

disobedience **(dis´ə bē´dē əns)**, *noun*, refusal to obey. Civil rights activists use nonviolent *disobedience* as a means to get laws changed.

disposition **(dis´pə zish´ ən)**, *noun*, one's natural way of behaving toward others. Students like Mr. Jefferson because he has a cheerful *disposition*.

disproportionately **(dis´prə pôr´shə nit lē)**, *adverb*, in a way that is out of relationship in size or number. Compared with other scientists, Dr. Lewis had a *disproportionately* high number of errors in his work.

disrespectful **(dis´ri spekt´ fəl)**, *adjective*, rude, impolite. The children wiggled and whispered and were *disrespectful* to the invited speaker.

distinctive (dis tingk´tiv), *adjective*, distinguishing from others; special. Her *distinctive* uniform showed that Despina was a member of the school marching band.

document (dok´yə mənt), *verb*, to provide evidence; to support with documents. James *documented* his identity by showing his passport and a driver's license with his picture. *noun*, a written or printed paper furnishing information; an official or legal paper. Your passport is a legal *document*.

draft (dräft), 1. *verb*, to select for military service. Many men did not enlist in the army or navy but were *drafted* for military service. 2. *noun*, a cool breeze. I felt a *draft* on my neck because the window was open.

effect (ə fekt´), *noun*, a result; something that is the consequence of a cause or action taken. We did not realize that the *effects* of our actions would be so serious. What we did affected many people.

ego (ē´ gō), *noun*, 1. a person's self. The harsh words of his friends hurt Mark's *ego*. 2. conceit; self-esteem. Bobby had a big *ego* and thought he was perfect.

egocentric (ē´ gō sen´ trik), *adjective*, self-centered and selfish. Trish is *egocentric*; she always thinks first about herself.

embrace (em brās´), *verb*, to take up or accept. Because Denise *embraced* causes without evaluating them, she had many disappointments.

emit (i mit´), *verb*, to give out. The hot metal *emitted* heat and light.

enactment (en akt´ mənt), *noun*, the act of enacting, or making into a law, statute, or regulation. The *enactment* of an amendment to the Constitution changes the law for the entire United States.

encampment (en kamp´ mənt), *noun*, a camp or camp site, especially one used by soldiers. The military *encampment* was near the river so that the soldiers could leave quickly in their boats in an emergency.

encounter (en coun´ tər), *noun*, an unexpected meeting. I had a chance *encounter* with my great-aunt while I was walking in the mall. *verb*, to meet unexpectedly. When Alberto *encountered* his friend at the mall, he was surprised to find him there.

encourage (en ker´ ij), *verb*, to give courage and hope; to urge on. We *encourage* students to complete their education.

endure (en dur´), *verb*, to put up with; to withstand something. Washington's army *endured* many days of poor food and little shelter.

engage (en gāj´), *verb*, 1. to keep busy or take part in. Marcel was *engaged* in that project for a long time. 2. to hire or employ. Louis and Clark *engaged* guides to take them across unfamiliar territory.

enlist (en list´), *verb*, 1. to join or volunteer for military service. Brian decided to *enlist* in the army. 2. to participate actively or engage in a cause; to sign up. Suzanne *enlisted* as a tutor to help students with their homework.

enterprise (en´ tər prīz´), *noun*, an important project or undertaking. The seeing-eye dog *enterprise* was an important venture.

entrée (on´ trā), *noun*, the main course of a meal. For their *entrée*, the guests chose chicken.

envision (en vizh´ ən), *verb*, to picture mentally. Morris Frank *envisioned* a world in which he could be independent.

epidemic (ep´ə dem´ ik), *noun*, a rapid spread of a disease in which many people are infected at the same time. Because so many school children contracted the flu, the scientists announced that there was a flu *epidemic*.

eradicate (i rad´ i kāt´), *verb*, to do away with. Insecticides were sprayed in a swampy area to *eradicate* the mosquitoes that were thought to carry the virus.

erupt (i rupt´), *verb*, to burst forth. The rumbling noise and release of steam indicated that the volcano was about to *erupt*.

etc. (et set´ ər ə), *Latin phrase* (abbreviation), see *et cetera*.

et cetera (et set´ ər ə), *Latin phrase*, and so forth. *Et cetera* is frequently used at the end of a list to mean there are more items than those listed. *Etc.* is the abbreviation for *et cetera*. I love blue things: blue sky, blue ocean, blue eyes, blue flowers, bluebirds, *etc*.

excavate (eks´ kə vāt), *verb*, to dig out. Millions of tons of dirt were *excavated* to build the Panama Canal.

except (ek sept´), *preposition*, other than. Howard likes everything about his new job *except* the Saturday hours.

excess (ek ses´), *noun*, an amount that is beyond what is needed or expected. The state collected more tax money than the legislature had expected, so the lawmakers were able to give the *excess* to local towns.

expression (ik spresh´ ən), *noun*, a phrase or word. 1. Because Mark did not know the idiomatic *expression*, he failed to understand the intended meaning. 2. a facial look. The questioning *expression* on the boy's face showed his lack of understanding.

exquisite (ek´ skwi zit), *adjective*, 1. beautifully and perfectly made; delicate. The tiny model of the ship was detailed and *exquisite*. 2. intense; sharp. Tatiana felt a stab of *exquisite* pride when she realized that her brother had won first prize in the debating contest.

extraordinary (ik strôr´dn er´ ē), *adjective*, beyond the ordinary. The beautiful painting was an *extraordinary* work of art.

extremely (ek strēm´ lē), *adverb*, very; much more than usual. The delicate object was also very heavy, which made it *extremely* difficult to handle.

fabric (fab´ rik), *noun*, cloth. The weaver wove a beautiful piece of *fabric* on his loom.

fanatic (fə nat´ ik), *noun*, a person who goes to extremes in advancing his or her cause. The *fanatics* tore down the building that housed the people they opposed.

fanciful (fan´sə fəl), *adjective*, quaint; fantastic; unreal. The tapestry was full of *fanciful* objects such as floating cows and purple grass.

fauna (fô´ nə), *noun*, animals in general or from a certain area. The *fauna* of America are different from the *fauna* of Africa.

faux pas (fō pä´), *noun*, a social blunder. Slurping his soup was an embarrassing mistake. David realized his *faux pas* when he saw people looking at him.

feature (fē´ chər), *noun*, a distinct part or quality; a characteristic. Clare's intelligence and her sense of humor are two of her most appealing *features*.

fiesta (fē es´ tə), *noun*, a festival or celebration. You can take part in *fiestas* in Mexico and many other places where Spanish-speaking people live.

filet mignon (fil´ ā mēn yôn´), *noun*, a tender and very choice cut of beef. Our *filet mignon* had no fat and was very easy to chew.

fleet (flēt), *adjective*, rapid; swiftly moving. Arabian horses are *fleet* runners.

fleeting (flē´ting), *adjective*, passing swiftly; moving swiftly away. Manuel got a *fleeting* glimpse of the car as it sped down the road.

flora (flôr´a), *noun*, plants in general or from a specific area. Tropical *flora* such as orchids need warm, moist climates in which to survive.

fluorescent **(flo͞o ə res´ənt)**, *adjective*, emitting light when exposed to some kind of radiant energy. *Fluorescent* tubes have a special powder inside that gives off light when electricity goes through them.

forefront **(fōr´frunt)**, *noun*, the most forward part; the part at the front. José likes to be in the *forefront* of the discussion when decisions are being made.

foremost **(fōr´ mōst)**, *adjective*, being the first in position, rank, time, or place. The *foremost* reason that I am voting for that candidate is her position on education.

foresee **(fōr sē´)**, *verb*, to see beforehand; to use foresight. Emma could *foresee* the time when she would enter college.

foresighted **(fōr´sīt ed)**, *adjective*, able to provide for the future. I would rather work with a *foresighted* person than one who knows everything in hindsight.

foretell **(fōr tel´)**, *verb*, to tell beforehand; to predict. We all wish we could *foretell* the future.

foul **(foul)**, *adjective*, 1. dirty, smelly. Because Justina slipped and fell in the mud, she returned home with a *foul* smell on her clothes. 2. wicked, vile. Our neighbor treated us in a *foul*, offensive manner by leaving his trash in our yard.

game **(gām)**, *noun*, 1. animals such as birds and fish that are hunted for sport or food. Many countries set aside preserves where hunting wild *game* is not allowed. 2. a sport or entertainment. The *game* of soccer is popular in many countries around the world. 3. *informal adjective*, ready and eager. The players were *game* to begin.

gem **(jem)**, *noun*, a precious stone, especially when cut and polished; a jewel. The jeweler showed us a collection of *gems* that could be set into rings.

geyser **(gī´ zər)**, *noun*, a spring that shoots up hot water. *Geysers* are found above areas of molten rock in the earth's crust. *Geysers* erupt from time to time, shooting hot water up into the air.

gorgeous **(gôr´jəs)**, *adjective*, splendid; richly colored. I thought that the tropical flowers were absolutely *gorgeous*, with glorious hues and fantastic shapes.

graphic **(graf´ ik)**, *noun*, a diagram, picture, or graph. The word *graphic*, used as a noun, is a newer form of the word. Margot created a computer *graphic* that had dozens of intersecting lines. *adjective*, clear and very distinct. My teacher painted a *graphic* picture of what would befall us if we failed to do our homework.

guise **(gīz)**, *noun*, a style of dress; appearance. The swindler appeared in the *guise* of a well-dressed, important person.

hacienda **(hä´ sē en´ də)**, *noun*, a large estate in Spanish-speaking countries. My friends live in a *hacienda* located in the rolling hills of Mexico.

harvest **(här´ vist)**, *verb*, to gather a crop. The farmer went to the field to *harvest* the wheat.

havoc **(hav´ ək)**, *noun*, great destruction. The tornado caused great *havoc* when it destroyed many houses

hazard **(haz´ ərd)**, *noun*, risk; exposure to harm. Crossing a busy street against a red light is an obvious *hazard*.

heritage **(her´ə tij)**, *noun*, what is handed down from one generation to the next. You may be able to trace your ancestors to learn about your *heritage*.

hinge **(hinj)**, *noun*, a joint on which a door, cover, or lid swings open or shut. The two shells, or valves, of an oyster or clam are fastened together with a *hinge*.

hitch **(hich´)**, *verb*, 1. *(informal meaning)*, to obtain a free ride. Simon was running late but was able to *hitch* a ride to school with his best friend's father. 2. to connect or attach one thing to another. The driver *hitched* our car to the back of his tow truck.

hole **(hōl)**, *noun*, an opening or hollow section through something. Lava or hot water can come up through the crust of the earth through vents or *holes*.

hue **(hyo͞o)**, *noun*, a color or tint. The artist preferred to use pale *hues* rather than dark colors.

identical **(īden´ tə kəl)**, *adjective*, the same. When placed next to each other, the pictures appeared *identical*.

illiteracy **(i lit´ ər ə sē)**, *noun*, the condition of not being able to read and write. Many educators are concerned about the level of *illiteracy* in the country because they know that those who cannot read and write well are at an economic disadvantage.

illuminate **(i lü´ mə nāt)**, *verb*, to throw light on. The lamp *illuminated* the room.

immoral **(i môr´əl)**, *adjective*, morally wrong; wicked. The conduct of people who are *immoral* does not conform to standards of good behavior.

immortal **(i môr´ tl)**, *adjective*, living forever; never dying. Some people must think they are *immortal* because they take terrible risks with their lives.

impose **(im pōz´)**, *verb*, to place upon and require. When the government *imposed* a tax on everyday staples such as tea and flour, the people protested.

impressive **(im pres´ iv)**, *adjective*, able to impress. The daring circus act was so *impressive* that it made me shiver.

incandescent **(in´ kən des´ ənt)**, *adjective*, glowing with heat. *Incandescent* lights have wires that glow when electricity passes through them.

incredible **(in kred´ə bl)**, *adjective*, beyond belief. I witnessed an *incredible* event, one that I could hardly believe was happening right before my eyes.

independent **(in´ di pen´ dənt)**, *adjective*, 1. self-governing. The people of India wanted to become an *independent* nation and not controlled by any other power. 2. self-supporting. By the time Trish was twenty-one years old, she was *independent*; she had a good job and was maintaining her own apartment. 3. self-reliant, relying on one self. I respect her for her *independent* point of view; she knows what she believes in and is not shy in expressing it.

indifferent **(in dif´ ər ənt)**, *adjective*, not caring; having no interest. The student stared into space, *indifferent* to what the teacher was saying.

indignity **(in dig´ nə tē)**, *noun*, an insult; something that dishonors one. Being ignored was an *indignity* and hurt Andy's self esteem.

indirectly **(in´də rekt´lē)**, *adjective*, not in a direct manner. The librarian tried *indirectly* to quiet the noisy people by putting his finger to his lips.

insecticide **(in sek´ ti sīd)**, *noun*. a substance that kills insects. When spraying *insecticide*, Owen was careful not to get it into his eyes.

inspect **(in spekt´)**, *verb*, to examine; to look over carefully. The building supervisor had to *inspect* the construction to make sure there were no errors or omissions.

inspection **(in spek´ shən)**, *noun*, examination. The *inspection* of the house showed termites were living in the walls.

inspirational (in´ spə rā´shə nəl), *adjective*, giving inspiration. Dr. King's talk was *inspirational* and gave the listeners the courage to continue.

interconnect (in´tər kə nəkt´), *verb*, to connect with each other. The links in a chain *interconnect*.

interconnection (in´tər kə nək´shən), *noun*, a state of being joined with someone or something. We found no *interconnection* between the two men, who appeared to function independently of one another.

intercontinental (in´tər kon´ tə nen´ tl), *adjective*, between two continents. The Isthmus of Panama is an *intercontinental* link between the continents of North and South America.

international (in´ tər nash´ ə nəl), *adjective*, between or among nations. An *international* trade agreement was made between the United States and the European Union.

intersect (in´tər sekt´), *verb*, to cross or cut through. A traffic light will be placed where the two roads *intersect*.

intervention (in´tər ven´ shən), *noun*, the act of coming between two parties as in an argument. I appreciated my friend's *intervention* because he solved a serious problem by making a good suggestion. The plants grew larger than normal without any human *intervention*.

invertebrate (in vûr´ tə brāt), *noun*, an animal without a backbone. Mollusks and worms do not have vertebrae or backbones; thus, they are classed as *invertebrates*.

iridescence (ir´ə des´ əns), *noun*, having a quality of displaying various changing colors. Pearls exhibit *iridescence* when they are rotated under a light.

irrefutable (i ref´ yə tə bəl), *adjective*, not able to be refuted or disproved. The facts were *irrefutable*; no one could deny or disprove them.

irritant (ir´ i tənt), *noun*, something that annoys or irritates. The dust is an *irritant* in my throat.

irritate (ir´ i tāt), *verb*, 1. to cause to become sore. Sand grains can *irritate* a clam's mantle. 2. to make angry or annoy. Alex was *irritated* when his friend showed up 45 minutes late.

irritation (ir´ə tā´ shən), *noun*, that which irritates. The powder that went up my nose caused an *irritation* that made me sneeze.

isolate (ī´ sə lāt´), *verb*, 1. to set apart from others. The scientist could not *isolate* the virus that caused the illness. 2. to quarantine. Because there were many sick people on the ship, the ship was *isolated* for two weeks and had to remain in the harbor.

isthmus (is´məs), *noun*, a narrow strip of land connecting two larger land masses. The *Isthmus* of Panama connects South America with Central America.

its (its), *possessive adjective*, belonging to it. The cat licked *its* paws.

it's (its), *contraction for it is* or *it has*. *It's* been a long day.

kinship (kin´ ship), *noun*, family relationship. The help that the four cousins give one another shows their strong *kinship*.

lasso (las´ ō) *noun*, a rope with a sliding noose at the end. The cowboy used a *lasso* to catch cattle and horses.

launch (lônch), *verb*, 1. to put into action. The governor *launched* an investigation to discover where the members of the council had gone wrong. 2. to lower a boat into the sea. The mariners *launched* several small boats to carry the passengers to the shore.

linguist (lin´ gwist), *noun*, an expert in languages. She is a *linguist* and knows a lot about the derivation of words.

lock (lok), *noun*, a part of a canal with door-like gates that can be opened and closed so that the water level can be raised or lowered in it. A canal *lock* allows ships to be raised or lowered to a different water level.

loner (lōn´ ər), *noun*, one who stands apart, without company. Male elephants sometimes become *loners* who do not associate with others of their kind.

lovelier (luv´ lē ər), *adjective*, more beautiful. Jane had never seen a *lovelier* string of pearls.

lucrative (lo͞o´ krə tiv), *adjective*, profitable. The music club found that selling baked goods was a *lucrative* activity that yielded enough money to pay for the club trip.

lumber (lum´ bər), *verb*, to move along heavily or clumsily. The heavily loaded camels *lumbered* along the rutted path. *noun*, timber cut into boards or planks. The carpenter bought *lumber* for the porch she was building.

luster (lus´ tər), *noun*, a gloss or bright shine. The large pearl shines with a lovely *luster*.

magnificent (mag nif´ ə sənt), *adjective*, splendid or grand; outstanding in all respects. Frank saw many *magnificent* rock formations when he visited the Grand Canyon.

maître d' (mā´ trə dē´), *noun*, headwaiter. The *maître d'* is the headwaiter of a restaurant and is in charge of all the waiters.

mantle (man´ təl), *noun*, 1. a loose sleeveless cloak. The shepherd in the fairy tale wore a woolen *mantle* over his shoulders. 2. something that covers or conceals. A *mantle* of dust covered the furniture. 3. a membrane that lines the inner surfaces of the valves, or shells, of mollusks. Oysters have soft *mantles* over their bodies. (Note: The shelf over a fireplace is commonly spelled mantel.)

marine (mə rīn´), *adjective*, of the sea. The seas have many kinds of *marine* life, such as fish and corals.

marine biologist (mə rīn´ bī ol´ə jist), *noun phrase*. *Marine biologists* study the organisms of the sea.

mariner (mar´ə nər), *noun*, a sailor; one who helps sail a ship. The *mariner* let out the sails, which filled easily in the strong wind.

massacre (mas´ə kər), *noun*, an indiscriminate killing of many. The soldiers fired into the crowd and caused a terrible *massacre*. *verb*, to kill many without regard for them. The poachers illegally *massacred* many elephants in order to get their tusks.

mesa (mā´sə), *noun*, a flat-topped hill with steep sides. The word *mesa* comes from the Spanish word for table; mesas have flat tops. As we drove across the American Southwest, we saw many *mesas*.

metaphor (met´ ə fôr´) *noun*, a comparison between two things that are essentially different, such as calling a storm "a dragon." Poets search for *metaphors* that express their feelings and ideas.

microphone (mi´ krə fōn´), *noun*, a device that can transform sound waves into electric currents. *Microphones* can now be made smaller than a pencil eraser.

midway (mid´ wā), *adverb*, halfway, in the middle between two points. Kansas is about *midway* across the North American continent.

mimic (mim´ ik), *verb*, to make fun of by imitating. The monkey *mimicked* the lady by putting her hat on just as she did.

mindful (mīnd´fəl), *adjective*, having in mind; aware. As she spoke, the candidate was *mindful* of the effect that her words were having on the crowd.

minimal (min´ə məl), *adjective*, least possible. The room had *minimal* furnishings, just a bed, a table, and one chair.

minuscule (min´ ə skyo͞ol´), *adjective*, very, very tiny; wee. I needed only a *minuscule* amount of paint to cover the tiny scratch on the side of the door.

misconception (mis kən sep´ shən), *noun*, a mistaken idea. Kareem was under the *misconception* that the job required him to speak only English; he also was required to speak Spanish.

misdirect (mis´ də rekt´), *verb*, to give wrong directions; to put a wrong address on. The package was *misdirected* so it went to the wrong address.

misgivings (mis giv´ings), *noun*, feelings of doubt. Carmen had some *misgivings* that she had promised to do too much in too short a time.

misinterpret (mis´ in tûr´ prit), *verb*, to interpret wrongly; to misunderstand. Be careful not to *misinterpret* another person's gestures; they may not mean what you think.

mobility (mō bil´ ə tē), *noun*, the quality of being mobile; being able to move. Motorized carts can improve the *mobility* of many people who are physically disabled.

mortal (môr´ tl), 1. *noun*, a person. Human beings are *mortals*. 2. *adjective*, sure to die. We are *mortal* and will not live forever.

mosey (mō´ zē), *verb* (*informal expression*), to move along in a leisurely manner. The three friends decided to *mosey* down to the candy store.

multinational (mul´ tē nash´ə nəl), *adjective*, involving several countries. Some trade agreements are *multinational* and include countries on several continents.

multitude (mul´ ti to͞od´), *noun*, a great number of people or conditions. Marty enjoyed a *multitude* of successes—one right after the other.

naïve (nä ēv´), *adjective*, unsophisticated; simple and unaffected. Because Betty was *naïve*, she did not realize that the others were making fun of her.

nasty (nas´ tē), *adjective*, mean; hateful. The salesperson must have been having a bad day and snapped at me in a *nasty* voice.

Nobel Peace Prize (nō bel´), *proper noun phrase*, an international prize awarded by the Nobel Foundation to recognize a contribution to world peace. President Theodore Roosevelt received the *Nobel Peace Prize* in recognition of his work in negotiating peace between Japan and Russia.

nonfunctional (non fungk´ shə nəl), *adjective*, not working. The water flooded the cellar because the pump was *nonfunctional*.

nonproductive (non´prə duk´ tiv), *adjective*, not producing. The carpenter's efforts were *nonproductive* until he came back the next day with the right tool for the job.

nonviolent (non vī´ə lənt), *adjective*, without violence. The crowd stood quietly and did not move. This action was a form of *nonviolent* protest.

nuisance (nū´ səns), *noun*, a person or thing that annoys of offends. Carl made himself a *nuisance* by constantly whining and complaining about the long drive.

offspring (ôf´ spring), *noun*, the young of living things. The young *offspring* of many mammals are usually fed by their parents.

omnipresent (om´nə prez´ənt), *adjective*, being present everywhere. Cell phones are really not everywhere, but sometimes they seem *omnipresent*.

outcry (out´ krī), *noun*, a cry of distress or anger. There was a loud *outcry* protesting the referee's decision.

outwit (out wit´), *verb*, to get the better of; to be too clever for. When playing chess, Fatema *outwitted* her opponents with clever moves.

overdo (ō´ vər dü´), *verb*, to do too much. If you *overdo* when you exercise, your muscles may ache the next day.

overwhelm (ō´vər whelm), *verb*, to be overcome completely. Janet felt *overwhelmed* by the amount of work she had to complete over the weekend.

oyster (oi´ stər), *noun*, a bivalve (two-shelled) mollusk with a rough, irregular shell. *Oysters* live in shallow water clinging to rocks.

palomino (pal1ə mē´ nō), *noun*, a horse with a tan coat and a cream-colored mane and tail. *Palominos* are popular horses for riding in parades.

panic (pan´ ik), *verb*, to lose control and be filled with unreasonable fear. When the big dog ran toward him, Adam *panicked* and ran out into the street traffic.

particle (pär´ ti kəl), *noun*, a tiny bit or amount of something solid. *Particles* of sand sometimes irritate a clam's mantle.

passionate (pash´ən it), *adjective*, dominated by strong emotion. The students were *passionate* about their ball team and came to every game, rain or shine.

pearl (pûrl), *noun*, a lustrous, highly valued mineral deposit made by an oyster. *Pearls* range in color from white to almost black.

peer (pir), *noun*, a person of the same rank; an equal. Molly likes playing stickball with her *peers*.

peeved (pēvd), *adverb*, fretful; annoyed; cross. Nicole and Sam were *peeved* that they were not invited to the party.

pension (pen´shən), *noun*, regular payments for long service. Some war veterans get special disability *pensions* to help with their expenses.

periodically (pir´ē od´ik lē), *adverb*, at regular intervals. The geyser Old Faithful erupts *periodically*.

petit fours (pet´ē forz´), *noun*, small, rich, glazed tea cakes. Our *petit fours* were covered with chocolate icing.

phenomenon (fi nom´ ə non), *noun*, a remarkable thing that impresses the observer. The Grand Canyon is a natural *phenomenon*.

phone (fōn), *noun*, a common, clipped form of the word *telephone*. Jesse wanted to know when I was getting off the *phone*. Phone is also a word element meaning "sound," as in *telephone* and *xylophone*.

pinto (pin´ tō), *noun*, a horse with spots of various sizes. The cowboy's *pinto* had irregular markings.

pit (pit), *noun*, a hole in the ground. The workers dug a deep *pit* in the street to bury the new water pipe.

plaza (plaz´ ə), *noun*, a public square. Large, open paved areas are sometimes called *plazas*.

poach (pōch), *verb*, to go onto someone's property to hunt game illegally. It is unfortunate that elephants have been *poached* illegally for their valuable tusks.

pod (pod), *noun*, a small school of whales, porpoises, or dolphins. Groups of any kind of cetacean—which is the scientific name for dolphins, whales, and porpoises—are called *pods*.

policy (pol´i sē), *noun*, a plan of action by a governmental body or political group. The group's *policy* was one of equal opportunity for everyone.

politics (pol´i tiks), *noun*, the activities of government. The college students were studying *politics* to understand how the government worked.

poncho (pon´chō), *noun*, a blanket-like piece of clothing worn over the shoulders with a hole for the head. The traveler carried a rain hat and a folded plastic *poncho* in case of bad weather.

posterity (po ster´ ə tē), *noun*, the generations of the future. We have to protect our environment for *posterity*.

postscript (pōst´ skript), *noun*, 1. an addition to a letter after the signature, generally indicated by the abbreviation PS. The writer wrote a *postscript* at the end of her letter to make a point that she had forgotten to put into the letter itself. 2. a later addition to a literary work. At the end of her book, the author added a *postscript* to explain two points that she wanted to develop further.

prank (prangk), *noun*, a playful trick. The *prank* Steve played on Craig was a bit of mischief that Craig soon caught on to.

precariously (pri kâr´ē əs lē), *adverb*, in a dangerously uncertain, risky manner. Roger tried to scale the rocky cliff without a safety rope. He ended up *precariously* perched on a jutting piece of rock.

preconception (prē kən sep´ shən), *noun*, an opinion formed beforehand. The eighth-grader had a *preconception* as to what high school would be like.

predate (prē dāt´), *verb*, to happen before; to precede. Sam's birthday *predates* mine by only seven days, making him just one week older than I am.

preliminary (pri lim´ə ner ē), *adjective*, coming before the main business or event. At the movies, *preliminary* events—previews of coming attractions and requests to turn off cell phones—take place before the main attraction, the feature film.

premise (prem´ is), *noun*, a statement assumed to be true. The original *premise* was that each member of the team would do his or her own part of the research project.

press (pres), *verb*, 1. to urge onward; to hurry. The jockey *pressed* the horse to run faster. 2. to be under pressure. The hikers felt *pressed* to reach the top of the mountain by mid-afternoon so they could return before dark.

prevalent (prev´ ə lənt), *adjective*, widespread. The many disease-carrying mosquitoes in the area made yellow fever *prevalent*.

principally (prin´ sə pə lē), *adverb*, mostly; above all. Jeremy was hired *principally* to deal with customers at the store counter.

proceed (prō sēd´), *verb*, to advance or continue. If they *proceed* now, they will be finished before dark.

production (prə duk´ shən), *noun*, a process or result of producing. The *production* of wheat was much higher when new and improved technology was used.

prohibit (prō hib´ it), *verb*, to forbid by authority. The law *prohibits* smoking in public places because it is a nuisance and a health hazard.

promote (prə mōt´), *verb*, to further; to contribute to the progress of. The advisors *promoted* the newer methods in agriculture.

pronto (pron´ tō), *adverb (informal expression)*, without delay. *Pronto* is slang from the Spanish word meaning "quickly." My friends told me to move, and *pronto*, to reach the arena in time for the game to begin.

pro-peace (prō pēs), *adjective*, for peace. Dr. Borlaug's activities in helping to reduce world hunger showed that he was *pro-peace*.

proverb (prov´ ərb), *noun*, a short, wise, old, and commonly used saying; a maxim. Benjamin Franklin coined the *proverb* "a penny saved is a penny earned."

purchase (per´chəs), 1. *noun*, something bought. The *purchase* Bob made cost him over 15 dollars. 2. *verb*, to buy. Bob had not intended to *purchase* such an expensive pen.

pursue (pər sü´), *verb*, to follow or chase to catch. The police *pursued* the bank robbers. Afterward, they *pursued* every lead that they found.

pursuit (pər so͞ot´), *noun*, the act of pursuing or going after. The immigrants came to America in *pursuit* of a better way of life.

quadrangle (kwod´ ran´ gəl), *noun*, a four-sided space. The college *quadrangle* has a building on each of its four sides.

quarantine (kwôr´ ən tēn), *verb*, to keep a person, plant, or animal apart or isolated from others for a time to prevent the spread of possible disease. When live cattle are brought into the country, they must be *quarantined* for some time to see if they are free of disease.

quartet (kwôr tet´), *noun*, a group of four. The singing *quartet* had two tenors and two basses.

radiate (rā´ dē āt´), *verb*, to spread rays or waves outward from a center. Cell towers, radio, and TV stations *radiate* energy waves.

recognition (rek´ əg nish´ ən), *noun*, 1. being recognized. *Recognition* came slowly; only after several hours had passed did my childhood friend realize who I was. 2. acknowledgment. The honor society gave Arlo an award in *recognition* of his fine academic record.

recount (ri kount´), *verb*, to give an account of. Myra *recounted* the events of the day so that we all knew what had happened.

reexamine (rē ig zam´ in), *verb*, to examine again. After Barbara complained of being in more pain, the doctor *reexamined* her hand.

rejoice (ri jois´), *verb*, to be filled with joy. The people *rejoiced* when they learned that their candidate had won the election.

relay (rē´ lā), *verb*, to receive something and send it on. Signals can be *relayed* from cell tower to cell tower to send messages over great distances.

relieve (ri ləv´), *verb*, to make easier; to bring or give relief. The driver stuck in a traffic jam was *relieved* when the cars started moving and she knew that she would get to her job on time.

remote (ri mōt´), *adjective*, far away, distant, isolated. Villagers living in *remote* mountain areas must travel a great distance to reach populated areas.

renege (ri neg´), *verb*, to go back on one's word. When asked to complete the task, Jared *reneged* on his promise and walked away from the work.

repellent (ri pel´ ənt), *noun*, something that repels or drives away. We used insect *repellent* when we walked down to the pond known to have a lot of mosquitoes.

repression (ri presh´ən), *noun*, act of holding down. The *repression* of free speech is a dictatorial act not allowed in a democracy.

repugnance (ri pug´ nəns), *noun*, distaste; aversion. Curtis looked with *repugnance* at the smelly trash that littered the street.

resent (ri zent´), *verb*, to feel angry at; to feel indignation at. We *resent* being made the object of other people's jokes.

reservoir (rez´ ər vwär), *noun*, 1. a place where water is stored. A *reservoir* formed when the engineers built the dam. 2. a large supply. The people of that country had built up a *reservoir* of good will across the world because of their generosity in the past.

residence (rez´ i dəns), *noun*, 1. a place where someone lives. A snail's *residence* is its shell. 2. the act or state of living in a place. The doctors were in *residence* at the hospital in India.

resist (re zist´), *verb*, to stand up against; to oppose. My friend *resisted* all my efforts to help her with her problem.

revolutionary (rev´ə lo͞o´shə ner´ ē), *adjective*, marked by extreme change. The changes brought about by the newer techniques of farming were *revolutionary*.

rodeo (rō´ dē ō´), *noun*, a show in which cowpunchers display their riding ability. Some riders were thrown off the bucking broncos at the *rodeo*.

rotary (rō´ tər ə), *adjective*, turning around as on an axis; having a part that rotates. Old *rotary* phones have a dial that you turn and release when it reaches each desired numeral.

rotisserie (rō tis´ ə rē), *noun*, a cooking device with a rotating rod or spit. The meat turning on the spit of the *rotisserie* emitted an inviting aroma.

RSVP, *abbreviation*. From the French *répondez s'il vous plaît*. (répon´dā sîl vo͞o plā´). RSVP translates as "respond if you please," but it really means that you should answer so that the host can plan on who is coming to the event.

scheme (skēm), *noun*, 1. a plan or program of action. The architect developed a *scheme* for expanding the kitchen that included complete drawings and a schedule of the work to be done. 2. a plot to deceive. The president of the corporation received a jail sentence for his *scheme* to take money from the company for his personal use.

scout (skout), *noun*, someone or something sent out ahead to get information. Sometimes robot airplanes are used as *scouts* to pick up signal or photo information.

selfish (sel´ fish), *adjective*, caring too much for oneself and not enough for others. It was *selfish* of Joe to grab the biggest and best slice of pie for himself.

serape (sə rä´ pā), *noun*, a blanket-like cloak made of wool. When not being worn, *serapes* are sometimes carried folded lengthwise over one shoulder.

series (sîr´ ēz), *noun*, a number of similar things happening in a row. We attended the first in a *series* of five band concerts.

service (ser´ vis), *noun*, 1. helpful aid or acts. Carla did me a great *service* by reminding me that our essay was due the next day. 2. the armed forces, i.e., army, navy, marines, air force. Some people who go into the *service* get training in highly technical skills.

shrivel (shriv´ əl), *verb*, to draw into wrinkles, especially due to lack of moisture. The plants *shriveled* up because they had not been watered in a long time.

simile (sim´ ə lē), *noun*, a creative comparison that relies on the word *like* or *as* to make the connection. *As good as gold* is an overworked *simile*.

simpleton (sim´ pəl tən), *noun*, a fool; a silly person. Only a *simpleton* believes that everything you read is true.

simultaneously (sī´məl tā´ nē əs lē), *adverb*, existing or occurring at the same time. An organist must use two hands and two feet *simultaneously* in order to play the instrument.

sly (slī), *adjective*, able to fool or deceive; tricky, wily. The *sly* pickpocket slipped his hand into Madge's bag and stole her wallet.

sombrero (som brâr´ ō), *noun*, a large hat with a broad brim and a large crown. Some Mexican musical groups wear fancy *sombreros* when they play traditional music.

sonar (sō´ när), *noun*, a device for locating underwater objects by reflection of sound waves. *Sonar* is an acronym for sound navigation and ranging.

soup du jour (so͞op´də zho͝or´), *noun phrase*, soup of the day. The *soup du jour* is the soup featured at a restaurant on a given day. Susanna chose the *soup du jour*—cream of broccoli.

spectacle (spek´ tə kəl), *noun*, a public show or display. The fireworks display was a grand *spectacle*.

spectacular (spek tak´ yə lər), *adjective*, making a great display. The marching band used *spectacular* patterns as part of its performance.

spectator (spek´ tā tər), *noun*, one who watches but does not take part. The *spectators* shouted their approval from the grandstands.

spew (spyo͞o), *verb*, to eject in a flow or stream. The volcano *spewed* lava down the mountainside.

spirit (spir´ it), *noun*, a feeling of; a sense of. The *spirit* of summer freedom filled the school in the last week of the school year.

submerge (səb mûrj), *verb*, to go underwater. Seals can jump into the water and *submerge* themselves to find food.

submerged, *adjective*, under the surface of the water. A ship can hit a *submerged* reef that its captain does not see.

subside (səb sīd´), *verb*, to move to a lower level; to settle down. The waves *subsided* as the storm passed on.

subsist on (səb sist´), *verb*, to live on or exist on. Some fish *subsist* on small organisms found near the shoreline.

substandard (sub´ stand ´ urd), *adjective*. below customary quality. The drinking water was considered *substandard* because the pollution level was above the level allowed.

substitute (sub´ stə tüt), *noun*, one person or thing taking the place of another. Carbonated drinks are not a healthful *substitute* for milk or water. *verb*, to take the place of another. It is not wise to *substitute* carbonated drinks for milk in one's diet.

substructure (sub´ struk´ chər), *noun*, a supporting structural part; a lower part of an object. The hull is part of the *substructure* of a ship.

superhuman (so͞o pər hyo͞o´ mən), *adjective*, beyond normal human ability. The group made a *superhuman* effort to get the gym decorated in time for the celebration.

superimpose (so͞o´ pər im pōz´), *verb*, to place something on top of something else. Adrian wanted to *superimpose* his map drawing on top of the wall poster to compare the two outlines of the North American continent.

supertanker (so͞o´ pər tang´ kər), *noun*, a very large ship used to carry liquids such as oil. The new *supertanker* had a double hull; it had two sides with a space in between to help prevent spills if the outside hull were damaged.

supervision (so͞o´ pər vizh´ ən), *noun*, the act of overseeing someone's work or activities. Expert *supervision* is needed for ships passing through narrow channels.

suppression (sə presh´ən), *noun*, the act of suppressing or prohibiting something. The citizens fought the *suppression* in a nonviolent way.

supreme (so͞o prēm´), *adjective*, greatest in importance or power. The king had *supreme* power over his subjects in ancient societies.

surname (ser´ nām), *noun*, last name or family name. Some *surnames* such as Carpenter or Forester come from an ancestor's occupation.

survive (sər vīv´), *verb*, to stay alive; to remain in existence. Few homes were able to *survive* the force of the hurricane.

table d'hôte (tä´ bəl dōt´), *noun*, a full course meal with a fixed price served at a restaurant or hotel. We did not care for the *table d'hôte* menu so we ordered a la carte. (Note: A synonymous phrase is *prix fixe*.)

tapestry (tap´ ə strē), *noun*, a fabric with designs or pictures woven into it. The Belgians are famous for weaving beautiful *tapestries* that people hang on their walls.

technician (tek nish´ ən), *noun*, one skilled in a technique. It takes a *technician* with special skills to work with living oysters.

technique (tek nēk´), *noun*, the procedure used to carry out a complex or scientific procedure. The teacher's skillful *technique* in using the microscope gave us a clear view of the organism.

technology (tek nol´ ə jē), *noun*, the methods, materials, and skills to carry out the building or development of complex products and systems. *Technology* has given us products such as automobiles and computers as well as advanced medical procedures.

telecom, *noun* (abbreviation), see *telecommunication*.

telecommunication (tell ə kə mū nə kā´ shən), *noun*, the exchange of thoughts and information at a distance. Almost instant *telecommunication* is in common use today. The *telecom* industry is important in many areas of the world today.

tercentennial (ter´sen ten´ ē əl), *noun*, a 300th anniversary. Also see *tricentennial*. A *tercentennial* celebrates an event that happened 300 years ago.

terminal (tûr´ mə nəl), *noun*, an end to a transport line. The ship reached the *terminal* where it was to be loaded.

their (thâr), *possessive pronoun*, possessive form of *they*, belonging to them. They put *their* books on the shelf.

there (thâr), *adverb*, in or at that place. Dora placed the chair over *there* by the piano.

they're (ther), *contraction* for *they are*. Pedro and Seema told me that *they're* definitely going to the movies tonight.

toil (toil), *verb*, to work hard. The climber *toiled* to reach his goal—the top of the mountain.

tortilla (tôr tē´ yə), *noun*, a flat pancake-like bread made from cornmeal and water. The *tortillas* were baked in an oven and rolled up with a vegetable filling.

tote (tōt), *verb*, to carry as a load. Helga and Jacques were able to *tote* their books in their backpacks.

toxic (tok´ sik), *adjective*, poisonous. Oil is *toxic* to sea animals and plants.

transfer (trans fûr´), *verb*, to shift from one person or place to another. After biting someone, a mosquito can *transfer* the disease organisms it picked up by biting someone else.

transform (trans fôrm´), *verb*, to change in form, function, or appearance. The caterpillar was *transformed* into a butterfly.

transit (tran sit´), *verb*, to pass through or over. Many ships have *transited* the Panama Canal.

transmission (trans mish´ ən), *noun*, the act of sending something from one person or place to another. The *transmission* of e-mail is a common activity today.

transmit (trans mit´), *verb*, to carry, or send, something from one person or place to another. Mosquitoes are able to *transmit* diseases.

transpire (tran spīr´), *verb*, to happen. Kyla was amazed at the number of events that *transpired* after she woke up Saturday morning—her sister let the cat out by mistake, her best friend phoned, and her father called her downstairs for breakfast.

travelogue (trav´ ə lôg), *noun*, a lecture, article, or film that describes a travel experience. After viewing the *travelogue* on China, I was determined to visit there.

trench (trench), *noun*, a long, narrow ditch. The workers dug a *trench* and buried telephone cables in it.

tricentennial (trī´ sen ten´ ē əl), *noun*, a 300th anniversary. See *tercentennial*.

trickery (trik´ ər ē), *noun*, the use of tricks to deceive or cheat. The con man used *trickery* to get the woman to withdraw money from her savings account.

trickster (trik´ stər), *noun*, a person who deceives or cheats. The West-African character Anansi was known as a *trickster* and a storyteller.

turning point (tûr´ning point), *noun phrase*, a point where an important change takes place. Graduation from high school was a *turning point* in Vic's life.

ubiquitous (ū bik´ wə təs), *adjective*, being present everywhere. Cell phones and laptop computers seem to be *ubiquitous*.

unable (un ā´ bəl), *adjective*, not able; not capable. The workers were *unable* to move the heavy iron beam without help.

unacceptable (un ak sep´ tə bəl), *adjective*, not to be accepted. The students' papers were *unacceptable* because they did not have proper paragraphs.

unduly (un dü´ lē), *adverb*, more than is due; excessively. The student felt *unduly* pressured because of all the homework assignments he had to complete in one night.

uneasy (un ē´ zə), *adjective*, disturbed; not comfortable. The negative statements made the audience feel *uneasy*.

unessential (un´ə sen´ shəl), *adjective*, not essential; not needed. Kendra left out an *unessential* part of the project because she felt that she had covered all the important topics.

unique (yü nēk´), *adjective*, only one of a kind; having no equal. The innovative invention was *unique*; there was nothing else like it in the entire world.

university (yo͞o´nə vûr´ si tē), *noun*, an institution of higher education made up of colleges and schools. After graduating from high school, Nora attended a *university* in South Dakota.

unrefined (un´rē fīnd´), *adjective*, 1. not processed. *Unrefined* oil is a mixture of many chemical substances. 2. crude. Some people appear *unrefined* because they fail to practice good manners.

untouchable (un tuch´ə bəl), *noun*, a member of the lowest caste in India. Some members of the upper caste in India do not want to touch the *untouchables*. The upper-caste people are very prejudiced if they believe that.

valve (valv), *noun*, 1. a device to control the flow of a liquid through a pipe. 2. a shell of a mollusk. 3. A structure in the heart to regulate blood flow. 4. a hinged lid inside an engine. *Valves* usually function by opening or closing.

vamoose (va mo͞os´), *verb* (informal expression), to leave in a hurry. *Vamoose* is slang from the Spanish word meaning "let's go." Sam yelled "*Vamoose*," when he realized that we had to move out quickly.

vehicle (vē´ ə kəl), *noun*, 1. a means by which something is communicated. E-mail is a popular *vehicle* for communicating. 2. a means of transporting something. A sixteen-wheeler truck is a very large *vehicle*.

vision (vizh´ ən), *noun*, 1. the ability to see; sense of sight. Ray's *vision* in both eyes is excellent. 2. the power of perceiving something by intellectual ability. Presidents need *vision* if they are to do their job well.

vista (vis´tə), *noun*, a distant view as seen from a window or other opening. The opening between the trees presented a magnificent *vista* of the valley below.

visual (vizh´ ü əl), *adjective*, having to do with sight. A dog's *visual* ability does not include color.

visually (vizh´ ü əl lē), *adverb*, in a way related to sight. Margot has been *visually* impaired since elementary school, but with eyeglasses her vision is quite good.

wee (wē), *adjective*, little, very small. Herb likes a *wee* bit of sugar in his tea.

wide berth (wīd bûrth), *noun expression*, lots of room or space because of some anticipated danger. Marvin gave the deep excavation a *wide berth* as he walked around it.

whole (hōl), *adjective*, complete; having all its parts. The *whole* class, all of the students, went to see the play.

winter (win´ tər), *verb*, to spend the *winter* in certain circumstances. Many birds *winter* in Mexico or other southern climates.

worthwhile (werth´ whīl´), *adjective*, worth the time, attention, or trouble. The chorus found that the time spent in extra rehearsal was *worthwhile*.

wreak (rēk), *verb*, to carry out with rage. The charging animal *wreaked* a lot of damage to the tent camp.

yearn (yern), *verb*, to feel a longing for. The slaves *yearned* for the time when they would be free.

yield (yēld), 1. *noun*, the amount produced. The *yield* of the farmer's apple trees that year was high compared to how many apples the trees produced in previous years. 2. *verb*, to produce an amount. The farm *yielded* a bigger crop after the farmer changed to a new kind of seed.

you're (yər), *contraction* for *you are*. "*You're* an excellent writer," I said to my friend Kyle.

Glossary by Dr. George Hennings, Professor Emeritus, Kean University, Union, New Jersey.

About the Author

Dorothy Grant Hennings is Distinguished Professor Emeritus, Kean University in New Jersey. She received her undergraduate degree from Barnard College, where she was elected to Phi Beta Kappa; her masters degree from the University of Virginia; and her doctorate from Teachers College, Columbia University. Before becoming a faculty member at Kean University, Dr. Hennings taught in the public schools of Rutherford and Fair Lawn, New Jersey. At Kean University, she taught courses in language arts and reading, children's literature, and developmental reading. She also spent considerable time mentoring student teachers in elementary school classrooms.

In 1992, the International Reading Association named Dr. Hennings as the recipient of the Outstanding Educator in Reading Award. In 1993, Hennings received the Distinguished Service Award from the New Jersey Reading Association. At Kean University, she was named Alumni Teacher of the Year in 1987 and was later recognized by the president of the University for her scholarly achievements.

Dorothy Grant Hennings is the author of many books. Her *Communication in Action: Teaching Literature-based Language Arts* is now in its eighth edition with Houghton Mifflin Co. Her *Reading with Meaning: Strategies for College Reading* is in its fifth edition with Prentice-Hall. She has authored other titles published by Scholastic, Goodyear, Teachers College Press, Phi Delta Kappa, Rand McNally, and HarperCollins. Hennings was an author on the Riverside Reading Series and has published articles in key journals including *Language Arts* and *The Reading Teacher.*